THE MORTGAGE PLAYBOOK

FOR MILLENNIALS

By Jeff Van Note,

The Mortgage Quarterback

The Mortgage Playbook for Millennials

Brought to you by The Mortgage Quarterback™ Jeff VanNote

GET in the GAME™

FROM THE AUTHOR

If I can ask one thing of you prior to reading this book, it is to contact any person you have had a conflict with in life, stemming from personal or business, and be the bigger person. Reach out to them, agree to disagree, and don't leave any bad blood or unspoken words. Life is too short, move on, and let go.

TABLE OF CONTENTS

FOREWORD:

By Mario Costanz

Passionate.

Undeniably Passionate.

Jeff Van Note's knowledge of the mortgage business is only surpassed by his passion for it. It is this passion that he puts to work in this timely, relevant and inspiring book that will keep you eagerly anticipating the next nugget of knowledge and the next interesting tidbit as you read through the chapters.

At a mid-point in my 20+-year career as an entrepreneur, I was briefly a mortgage banker during the mid 2000's. When Lehman Brothers collapsed and the real estate bubble burst in 2008, the mortgage investors I was working with were no longer able to fund even the full documentation loans that were originating out of my tax practice. So I left banking. And as a real estate developer, I still needed to get some condos I had built sold off so I had started an arduous process of finding lenders who could finance our buyers. It was then that I met Jeff as he details graciously here in this book.

Jeff had a confidence, even at the age of 21, which I admire to this day. Now, many in the mortgage business also have a can-do attitude, will work hard for their clients and are excellent salespeople. Some, however, have great confidence that is more akin to snake oil sales. As a lifelong New Yorker and entrepreneur, I've seen lots of snakes in business. And at first I was slightly skeptical that Jeff's confidence might be hiding something. I'm Happy to admit that that initial bit of skepticism was 100% wrong. Jeff is as authentic as they come, he tells it like it is and even back then when he was just starting out, he knew the mortgage business better than most of his colleagues' decades older than him.

Although I am not a Millennial myself, the words written here words ring true for any generation including my own, Gen X. The trials and tribulations that Jeff details will help you take the guesswork out of building your own solid financial foundation in real estate whether it be owning your own home or building an empire of investment properties.

I have watched Jeff transform from a young kid navigating in a vicious real estate market into a true leader in his profession who has helped countless people to finance their properties and to turn their hopes and dreams into reality. Whether you choose to read this book and use it as inspiration for a career in mortgages, real estate and investing or utilize the knowledge presented here to help you prepare for your own primary residence purchase; following Jeff's advice will save you countless headaches, mistakes and potentially tens of thousands of dollars. Even better for you would be if you had the opportunity to work with Jeff on the financing of properties for yourself or your clients.

Jeff is a rare breed in today's maze of corporate order takers who instead will figure even the most challenging scenarios out and go to the end of the earth for his clients, his friends and his family. He is a wonderful mix of a strong work ethic, compassion, a never give up mentality and an ability to think outside the box.

At Happy Tax, one of our primary responsibilities as a franchisor is leading, coaching and supporting our franchisees. It could be said that a quarterback provides the same to his team. Jeff's experience and teachings exude these attributes and he has truly earned the right to be called the Mortgage Quarterback. Following Jeff's journey will guide through some funny moments, hard lessons, heartwarming stories not to mention every bit of what you most likely picked this book up for, your complete playbook to everything you need to know about mortgages and real estate financing.

Always Remember: There is Always a Way! ;)

Sincerely,

Mario Costanz

CHAPTER 1:

INSIDE THE HELMET

I, Jeff VanNote, entered into the mortgage industry at a time when no one else was, at the tender age of 20. In fact, 90% of the industry was getting out, the mortgage market was collapsing, home values were tanking, and no one could access money. Redirecting my life from the football field to the mortgage field was easy, as I applied the same values learned on the gridiron, of hard work, dedication and commitment, quickly propelled me forward in an industry that was lacking honesty, integrity, heart, and most importantly, FUN. My biggest accomplishments in my first 10 years are winning "40 under 40" Most Influential mortgage people in the country, all while under 30, closing $31 million dollars in loans in my second full year in the business, and helping over 1,000 clients obtain mortgages for their real estate. What I am most proud of are the relationships I have formed with realtors, attorneys, and clients along the way, simply by doing the right thing and proving to be a valuable, reliable source.

My mission is very clear. My mission is to educate consumers, especially Millennials, about Mortgage Lending & Real Estate, in order to prevent the 2008 Real Estate Market collapse and financial markets meltdown from happening ever again.

My *why* is very meaningful. I witnessed hundreds of people per year from 2008 until about 2012 lose their homes, destroy their credit, and have their families break apart due to financial hardships, mostly stemming back to not being able to afford their high mortgage balance and loan payment, along with excessive household debt.

With the proper implementation of early mortgage and real estate education to kids in High-school and college, even post college, I believe the potential for another 2008-like crisis can be significantly reduced, while having our future home owners make much more educated and calculated risk decisions.

It was December of 2007; football season had just come to an end after losing to the University of Massachusetts in the Division 1aa playoffs. It was a great year for us Fordham Rams, having won the Patriot League Championship. On a personal level, I didn't play as much as I had expected to, but wound up starting quite a few games on special teams. The next year was going to be it—my break out year. Just not on the football field.

For the previous 5 months, I would walk home every day from class and practice and training, passing the same house on the right side of the street. The house had a "FOR SALE" sign, and it was listed with a realtor from "RE/MAX VOYAGE". Since I was familiar with the mortgage business, and heard of these loans where you didn't need any income, credit or assets, I figured just maybe I would be able to buy this house, for the right price, and rent out the house to my teammates or other college kids, and make money. I called the realtor's number almost every day for 5 months. I sent emails, text messages, yet no reply, ever. Finally, on one December day, when I had some time off, I decided to put a suit and tie on, and drive to this realtor's office. It was in the Bronx, so how far could it really be? An hour and a half later, I was there. The funniest thing was, had I gone the back way, I would have been there in 20 minutes. But, at the time, the navigation systems were terrible if you remember. Anyway, I got there, ready to rock and roll. I parked on the street in front of the office, and the office looked like it was on the second floor. So be it. I walked up the stairs, walked in, saw the friendly receptionist, and said, "Hey, I'm Jeff. I am here to inquire about the house for sale on Crotona Avenue"... "Honey, that house ain't for sale," I was told. So, me being me, questioning everything, I said, "Well then why is there a FOR SALE sign on it?" I was then informed the house was a short sale, and there was a squatter (one who illegal resides in a property without any rights) was in the basement. I was confused but figured hey, let me just leave my business card, which at the time, I had from interning at my father's mortgage company, Jersey Mortgage Company. The receptionist looked down at the card as I had begun to walk out and she said, "Hey, you do mortgages?" Talk about a deer in headlights. I said "Yeah"... She then handed me 2 pieces of paper, "these are two people that called up today looking for mortgages... here give them a call". I took the paper and walked out of the office, thanking her as I left.

As I get back into my car I thought to myself, now what do I do? I don't really know mortgages, and I never planned on doing mortgages. To make a long story short, I went back to that office every single day from the next day to June of 2009. 19 months straight. I would get up in the morning, work out, maybe attend some college classes, hit spring practice, and in-between, sometimes during classes, or after classes, I would drive over to their office, now the short way, and just say hello, check in, grab food, drop off pizza, and just say hello. It was easy; I became friends with everyone in the office. In

> **Tip #1**
>
> Text your best friend. Ask them if they want to invest in your future together. If they say yes, tell them it's game on, and let's buy property together. Buy a nice house, live together, and rent out the other rooms to friends.

particular, I became best friends with the Broker Owner of Re/Max Voyage, Andrew Fernandez, who at the time was the youngest person, especially broker/Owner, second to me! And he was… 29. He and I hit it off pretty quickly. We spent many nights together, sitting in the car, brainstorming, thinking big picture, and really getting to know each other. So much so that I was invited to his sister's wedding in The Bahamas that summer. I closed nearly 40 deals in the first 18 months just out of his office alone, which I had been working hard for. Andrew and I had a very interesting relationship, built on business, but turned into a true friendship. We spent some holidays together, as my family was in New Jersey, and often times "duty called" and I wouldn't be able to make it home, or had to leave and come back to the Bronx early. Andrew was a big brother to me, along with a friend that was equal, simultaneously a large referral source, which I worked extremely hard to gain his respect, and trust, but more importantly his friendship. I asked Andrew in 2008 two questions, "Why do mortgage people always leave the Bronx," and "Why do they always disappear in general?" his answers to me were simple, "They couldn't handle the Bronx way of business, and everyone wanted to go to Westchester, with nicer people and bigger loan amounts."

Having no real knowledge of the Bronx, the business, or the industry, I just shrugged my shoulders and nodded I understood. In the spring of 2008, my football coach called me into his office the day before our spring game. Now, I was running with the starters. This means that I had a great shot at significant playing time in the up and coming season. I was strong, fast, and knew the playbook inside and out. I went into my evaluation meeting ready for great news, excited about getting on the field in the fall. "Jeff, I appreciate your work ethic, but you're not my player and our team is headed in a different direction. We are going to have a rebuilding year and get younger guys on the field to show off their skill set". I sunk in my chair. We had just received our Fordham Championship rings, which we all wore proudly. So proud that it was often the topic of conversation when I met with clients, realtors, attorneys… you name it. It looked like a Super Bowl ring, and people respected it. I felt the life fall right out of me. Devastated, emotional and slightly immature, I said, "Fine, give me my transfer papers." My coach agreed and handed me them.

Now, remind you, the spring game was the next morning. Literally we had our spring game, where all alumni come back to Fordham to watch us play against each other, offense vs. defense, maroon vs. white. I got in my car, drove home to my mom's house. I told both of my parents not to come to the game tomorrow. If you know my parents, they are the most loving and supportive out there, but they won't pry or ask questions unless I offer the information. I am pretty sure I lay in bed at my mom's house for hours, crying, thinking, tossing and turning. I was hurt, defeated. My dreams were cancelled. I spent the last 3 years at Fordham working day in and day out. Getting up at 5 am for winter workouts, summer strength and conditioning programs, heavy weight lifting, you name it; all to have my world come crashing down. I didn't sleep at all that night… I couldn't sleep. For the first time in my life, I had no control over something that provided so much fun, excitement, and purpose since I was 5 years old. Football. Not being able to lie in bed any more, it was about 5:45am, I got up and said "I am playing in this Spring Game today, whether they like it or not." I drove all the way back to the Bronx, over an hour's drive, listening to a mixtape I'd made with Puff Daddy,

> **Tip #2**
>
> If you want more of a tax refund, buy a home and take out a mortgage loan. Your mortgage interest paid annually is tax deductible. Speak to your accountant or a CPA about just how much you'll increase your refund and reduce your income tax by.

Mase and Lil Jon on it. I was going to show these people how much of a mistake they made. I walked into the locker room, strictly business. Headphones on, game ready. I ended up leading the game with catches, receiving yards, and touchdowns. After the game, I walked up to the coach and extended my hand, "coach, please, reconsider your choice"... "Our choice is made, good luck".

Deflated once again, I knew I left the field that day with everything I had to give, on the field, including my heart and purpose.

Luckily, I had busted my butt with the Re/Max Voyage relationship for the previous 5 months, so whatever, I will go make some real money for myself. I will go out and get some mortgage business, really help people get approved, and have realtors close deals much quicker with my level of service and growing knowledge, it's a no brainer. So, that's what I did. From the football turf to the concrete jungle, I applied the same commitment, dedication, work ethic and drive to make a name for myself very quickly in the industry. The only problem was, I never felt fulfilled. Now, at the time, I was going to Fordham for football and girls... sorry Mom and Dad, I mean Finance and marketing, right, financing and marketing. So, I applied "finance" with mortgages, and "marketing" to market myself, to gain people's attention and advertise deals I had gotten closed. It was great! I pretty much stopped going to classes. I would maybe go to two or three per semester, maintaining my 1.8 GPA, skipped out on some finals, midterms, you name it. I really didn't care at this point; I felt Fordham screwed me on the football field, so I'll screw them on their graduation rate. Really mature, right?

Anyways, the business was getting tougher and tougher. Realtors were becoming more desperate and everyone began asking for kickbacks, which I still to this day have never done. Finally in June of 2009, I threw my hands up in the air and said, "I am done." I spent the next 45 days training hard, real hard, to get myself in shape to be able to get back onto the field. I wound up going to a small Division 3 school in Pennsylvania, got myself on the field for some plays, and ended up tearing my rotator cuff. That day I tore my shoulder, I moved back home, dropped out of school, and that was that.

While laying home in bed, recovering from surgery, I received a call on December 8, from Andrew Fernandez. Now, Andrew and I had never lost touch. We text, we emailed, we stayed in touch on a personal level like no other. "Mr. VanNote... Let me ask you something..." "What's up Bro?" I replied. "Do you think you can close a deal for me by Christmas?"

Chuckling, I replied, "I am out of the game. However, if I was still in it, of course, you know I can close a deal as quickly as you need to" "Do you think maybe you can call this client Miss Caprio? She just had her loan denied by Bank of America, and it is my listing and sale. The sellers are elderly and are very upset, my client is upset, and if anyone can do this my brother, it is you". After a few second pause... and lightning speed thinking I came back with "Give me her number, I will call her right now. If I can do the deal, I will have it closed for you BEFORE CHRISTMAS." "Now that's the JVN I know," Andrew stated.

So, I went on to call Miss Caprio, dissected the reason Bank of America denied the loan, which was common, restructured the entire scope of the loan that night, downloaded my mortgage loan software for my Dad's company,

> **Tip #3**
>
> Do NOT trust the accuracy of Zillow's Zestimates or proposed mortgage payments.
>
> **Tip #4**
>
> If your parents gift you money for your primary resident purchase, there are ZERO tax implications for either you or them.

and submitted the loan the following morning, December 9th. I was back in the game. That day, I drove all the way to the Bronx to pick up all of Miss Caprio's documents, as I learned in the past, the only way to get things done are to do them yourself, and hand deliver a full loan package into the underwriter's office, and not leave the office until the commitment was issued. The loan was committed that day, December 9th; the same day the loan was submitted.

Now let's unravel my thought process behind this as to what was on the line. First, it is a tremendous rush of excitement having the ball (the loan) in my hands, with the game on the line (the real estate transaction's outcome) with a clear site of the end zone (the closing of the deal) and the weak defenders (time, attorneys, sellers, etc.) in the way of me scoring a touchdown. Second, we have a family that wants to close on their house before Christmas and the New Year, the emotional pressure and stress alone is unfathomable, unless of course you have personally been in this situation. You have elderly people who need the money for personal reasons who now have an unknown and worry of potentially starting all over again. And finally, my dear friend has his real estate commission on the line, and everyone can use an extra $10k or so, especially around the holidays.

Now for the good news, we closed this loan December 23, 2009. We did the unthinkable. Talk about reliving the glory days (Which at this point had only been gone six months). I truly missed the pressure, the rush, the interactions, and most importantly, the delivering of the impossible. Helping people has always been my passion, and turning a bank's "NO" into my bank's "GO" is truly one of the most amazing feelings in the world.

While I was driving to the Bronx that day, December 9, I left out that I had called my friend Mario up, who just had a baby, to check in and catch up, along with letting him know I was back in action again. He asked if I wanted to drive down to Virginia with him, to meet a guy by the name of John Hewitt, the following week. Mario was looking to turn his private tax practice into a franchise, like an H&R Block, or Jackson-Hewitt, and Liberty Tax seemed to be his most desirable option. I took him up on the offer, to spend some quality time and catch up on what I missed in the prior 6 months in the Bronx market. He picked me up a week later at my mom's house and off we went to Virginia and back in the same 24 hours. What came out of that trip was a partnership, with me putting up my life savings into buying a liberty tax franchise, which I could then cross market mortgage business from tax clients, and vice versa. It was a no brainer. So, we did just that. We opened up a brand new office, did the full gut rehab build out, signed the lease, and we were open and ready for tax season. Talk about being thrown to the wolves, we had to interview people, hire people, manage people, monitor people, all while bringing business in, all of which I had never done before. I spent hours and hours watching marketing videos, management videos, how to hire videos, and pretty much got no sleep from January-April of 2010. For the first month, I would wake up every day at 5am at my mom's house in Branchburg NJ, and drive all the way to the Bronx, and then back to her house at 11pm, shower, sleep and do it all over again, until I got myself an apartment at a past client's house in their basement. Yes, I rented an illegal apartment, in a basement, where I lived for well over a year. It was cheap, $900/month. I literally just slept there, as the rest of my time was spent working and building business, with an occasional Thursday night flag football game in Brooklyn.

Tip #5

If you are afraid of buying real estate due to commitment or fear of the unknown, I recommend you take a real estate course or mortgage lending course to educate yourself.

After tax season, and dealing with some personal headaches with relationships with a lot of realtor referral sources, a friend of mine asked me if I could set up a meeting with him and Mario. Mario was your serial entrepreneur, before anyone ever even used the word entrepreneur. Mario had his real estate broker license, was a small real estate developer, used to do mortgages, did credit repair, had a pizza shop, you name it, he did it. So, I did just that. I made the introduction between current real estate sales person, and Mario. I attended the meeting just so both would feel comfortable. What came out of the meeting was an opportunity to help own and set up a real estate office. Mario and I combined, between mortgages and taxes, had over 1,500 clients. The nice thing about real estate is, everyone needs it. The licensed sales person at the time was just getting started and wanted to own his own business. Together, we decided we would open up a RE/MAX franchise, where I would put up the money and get the mortgage business in return, as well as help with sponsorships and marketing, and any other expenses if they came up. We owned and operated this franchise for a few years and then one day there was a massive falling out, and the my 2 partners never spoke again. Being caught in the middle, I took a step back and let them resolve the issues, which inevitably led to a sale of the franchise to an already established RE/MAX Broker and brand.

Meanwhile, we were still flipping properties. The two properties that came to mind were my first and last ones in the Bronx. The first one was 736 Prospect Street, which I bought for $135,000, and it was a complete shell. A shell is when the entire inside is ripped out and demolished, basically the outside looks the same, but the inside is an empty box. I waited to buy this property for almost 2 years, as it was a short sale. When I finally closed, I went into the property and found a squatter living in it. The guy was from Puerto Rico and had naked pictures of girls hanging up in his bedroom (by "bedroom" I mean empty room with clothes on the floor which he would sleep on). He felt it necessary to go to the bathroom, on the floor, in his bedroom, since the plumbing didn't work in the bathrooms, again because the house was a shell. Being just 24 years old, I didn't feel like engaging with a homeless squatter, but the house needed to be cleaned out. I found some kids walking on the street and paid them $250 to clean the entire house out and throw out all of the garbage, clothes, and clean up the backyard, and told them I would give them another $250 when they were done. And I did just that. I went back in the house and the thing was spotless. We then listed the house on the market and sold it for $185,000, making a quick $50,000, that went right back into the businesses, both the liberty tax and re/max.

The last property I flipped in the Bronx was 1535 Vyse Avenue. The thought of this address still makes me want to throw up. We bought this property for $285,000. According to the bank-owned records and title report, it was a legal four-family that had been foreclosed on. Great, right? Yup. Now, we get a licensed contractor estimate for about $125,000 or so dollars. Hi ho hi ho, off to work we go. The place wasn't in bad condition at all; it just needed a lot of TLC, with a new boiler, new floors, and redone bathrooms and kitchens. The set up was an interesting lay out, where it appeared there were actually five units in the building, but the records said legal four family. My main job was to make sure the taxes and insurances were paid, along with the contractor. About eight months into the project, we were told that the work was fully completed, so, I decided to go to the property, as I had only been there to let people in and out when needed. Turns

Tip #6

Make sure you take out a nice size life insurance policy when you buy a home to cover the entire balance of the loan and then some extra to give to your family. Don't leave your loved ones with debt in case of an emergency or tragedy.

out the bathrooms were done improperly, where the vanities were too big and actually stuck out blocking the door ways, the floors were warped and slanted, where if you put a ball at the top of the floor, it was slide down, the entire floors were slanted on a large angle.

I immediately called my partner Mario up and it was a disaster dealing with the contractor. His words were "I put make up on a pig" which basically means he did everything cheap, and wrong, and we were stuck. So, we had to hire another contractor to come in and pretty much do all of the work all over again, which wound up costing us nearly $35,000 more than expected. Now let's get to the real fun part. We finally completed all of the work and we were ready to get the certificate of occupancy, which gives us final approvals and sign offs that the work was done right and now we can either sell or rent the property. The inspection window was from 9 am-3 pm, so, in order to make sure this happened, I drove to property and parked out front. I got there at 8am, to make sure I was there in case they came early. Here is the best part—I didn't leave there until 9PM. Why? Well, the buildings inspector kept saying he was coming, he got delayed, etc, and then, never showed. That is right, he never showed. I was a lunatic, calling every single person I could to complain, to no avail. They rescheduled me for what turned out to be the day after Sandy hit. If you remember Hurricane Sandy in 2012, well, my inspection was for the day after it initially hit. Guess what? It got cancelled, again. At least this time, well in advance. The final inspection didn't get done until MARCH of 2013. Five months later. The buildings department said they were backed up and couldn't make it, and emergency repairs and requests were taking precedent. At this point, we had taken out a hard money loan on this and every month we had a $5,000 payment due. The buildings department single handedly cost us $25,000 in delays due to their negligence. Once the property was fully completed with a certificate of occupancy, we were able to rent the entire building out for $7,000 per month, which covered our hard money loan, our insurance, and taxes monthly. We saw a small profit but not enough to make sense to keep the building. Our loan amount was too high to refinance so we decided to sell the property. After 6 months or so of having the property listed, we sold the property for $515,000 all cash. Mario and I walked away with maybe $9,000 each or so, but a wealth of knowledge, and a great story.

In the summer of 2013, I broke into the Manhattan market place, and began doing a fair amount of mortgage business. I met some great people, mostly in the real estate start up world, who I became friends with. I spent every Tuesday and Thursday in the city, training realtors on mortgages, and getting to know them. In January of 2014, I moved back to my home state of New Jersey. I landed in Hoboken NJ with a friend. At that point I decided to market myself in both NY and NJ. I saw the way the market and prices were headed and believe NJ would start to see the same growth that NY was seeing, but over time. I was right. NJ became one of the hottest markets, and still to this day, is rapid increasing along the Hudson River waterfront, and surround areas, which I like to call "Manhattan's Backyard".

Since I had no experience in the market where I was living, I decided to rent, which I did for more than two years. I wanted to learn the area, see buying trends, learn the psychology and mentality behind buyers and borrowers in the market, and then, make a confident decision on purchasing. In February of 2016, I found a great condo in Jersey City heights. Jersey City

Tip #7
Buy a house with less money down and keep the rest of your money in the bank. Too many people put a large unnecessary down payment and leave themselves without an emergency fund for repairs.

Heights looks down on Hoboken, is up on a hill, and from various points, you can see the entire New York City sky line. The price of this condo was $350,000, which was way under market in my opinion. The listing with the realtor was advertised as "must be sold all cash." When I called the realtor, I inquired why it was necessary and he gave some indirect and non-helpful reasons. Long story short, I told him I worked for a mortgage company and could get the deal done. That day, I entered into contract, at $350,000, and a few months later I closed. One year later, in July of 2017, the same condo appraised, was valued, at $440,000.

Based on what I had seen in the NYC market place, specifically Brooklyn, I saw what was happening here in New Jersey. Spotting trends, forecasting visions and following the market from both the real estate and lending sides has proven to be very valuable. I fell in love with "The Heights", and wound up buying another condo here in the area, also under market value.

In January of 2017, I was fortunate enough to be offered the opportunity to re-join Residential Home Funding, whom I had worked for in the past for about a year. They allowed me to open an office for them in Hoboken, to create our blue print for success. My model was to hire millennials, specifically those outside the industry. This led to the hiring of my dear friend, and former real estate recruiter, Zack Evans. He came on board in July of 2017 as our realtor relationship director, and we hit the ground running. We first launched TheNextBK.com, which is a side-by-side comparison of Bushwick in Brooklyn, and Jersey City Heights. This site allows our New York clientele, and other individuals looking for real estate opportunities to see on paper, facts and trends. We believe the Hoboken and Jersey City Heights, and even Union City market places are "The Next Brooklyn."

Soon after this site was launched, we invented an app and a company called Home Buyer Huddle. Home Buyer Huddle is still in the early stages of development, but the app is now on both the Apple Store and Google Play store. The goal of Home Buyer Huddle is to provide consumers with accurate information and proper education on the real estate and lending market places. We believe a company like Zillow does more harm than good, and truly deceives consumers and shakes down realtors and lenders to charge excessively high fees to market themselves. Home Buyer Huddle's aim is also to give back 20% of all future profits, along with raising money for organizations like the Boys & Girls Club, Veterans, and the homeless. On December 21, 2017, we held our first annual Holiday Huddle in Hoboken, and raised over $13,000 and well over 200 toys and stuffed animals for the kids. Our model for Home Buyer Huddle also was created to inspire the youth to pursue career opportunities in anything real estate related, whether it be mortgage lending, real estate, appraisal services, home insurance provider, or even a property flipper. It is never too early to begin in this field, and it is especially never too early to learn about real estate or future streams of income. The entire industry is old and outdated, with the average realtor now 53 years old, according to the National Association of Realtors, across the US, and an average age of nearly 58, as a mortgage loan officer, according to the Mortgage Bankers Association. The market needs to get younger, and we believe we, my team and I, are going to be the ones to help do that by making real estate fun and exciting, along with using a social community and new technologies to do so.

Our belief as a company, and certainly mine personally, is that the

> **Tip #8**
>
> Always check to see if the property you are interested in is in a flood zone prior to putting an offer in. Flood insurance can be very expensive.

opportunities for millennials are endless. We want to show everyone that millennials can and will be the best generation ever to live, but it starts with their mentors and role models properly educating and inspiring them, and keeping them out of harm's way and unnecessary risk.

THE REAL estate Roller Coaster

First Time Home Buyers—Ups, downs, and some where in the MIDDLE.

GET READY FOR THIS. THIS IS REAL.

"YIKES"

"We have to move. We have to tell our landlord. Our parents don't think we should buy. We should be married first. What if we don't get approved? Do we have enough money? How do we get the best interest rate? What type of loan should we get? How much should we put down? Are we even ready to buy? Should I pay off my debt first? Is my credit score high enough? What if I lose my job, can my partner make the payments? What if I want to have a baby, can my husband handle this on his own? What if we don't like the house? What if we don't like our neighbors? HOW LONG IS MY COMMUTE GOING TO BE FOR WORK?"

"YIKES" "Am I, are we, really ready to do this?"

Yes, YOU ARE READY.

If you wait until the absolute right time to be "ready", you will never be ready. Take a chance. Take a Leap of faith. Trust that your team comprised of your mortgage lender, your realtor, your attorney, and your insurance company have your back!

You are going to be nervous. You are going to be anxious. You are going to question whether you are making the right move from day 1, to the day you close on your property and get your keys. You probably will be questioning it even after you get your new home. You are going to be happy. You are going to be excited. You are going to be scared. Heck, you may not even be able to sleep at night.

YOU are making probably the largest purchase or financial decision in your life. And you most likely will have this decision stick with you for 30 years, or longer.

Take a deep breath. Get your shit together. Get your team behind you.

Now is the time. Rates are going to go up. Prices will continue to rise. Don't be late to the party. You may just not get in.

REAL (LIFE) ESTATE STORIES

The years of 2008-2009 specifically turned out to be the best training for structuring mortgage loans that anyone could have ever gone through. As the guidelines were changing daily, if not by the minute, as more bank losses were occurring, it was like trying to hit a moving target. While learning on the fly and by the seat of my pants, I figured out a lot of the game at an early age. I was on a mission not only to close deals, but figure out how to close deals other lenders couldn't do, with one specific word in mind; creatively.

Fraud was running rampant in the mortgage business as it had for many years. Lenders were desperate, builders and property flippers were paying off appraisers to appraise property values much higher than their actual worth, creating straw buyers (straw buyers are someone who is paid to purchase a property under their name, usually with an FHA loan, or a low down payment loan, and say they are occupying the property as their primary residence, when they have no intentions of living there or moving in at all), some lenders even went as far as making fake tax returns, bank statements, credit reports, and pay stubs, and submitting them to the bank for approvals. There was a 4506 form, which verified tax returns with the IRS, but lenders didn't ever actually use them, plus banks were making so much money, they didn't care, as long as loans were being submitted and closed, people became reckless. When the bottom fell out of the market, the true value was in having banks to lend money, having investors in the secondary market to sell loans to, and be able to do deals directly in house, as a direct lender. A direct lender is a mortgage lender that can underwrite FHA, VA, and conventional loans in-house, approve them, lend their own money, close the loan, and then sell the loan (if wanted to) in the secondary market, for a profit, to a loan servicer. The secondary market became very strict, as apparently 80% of all delinquent loans, came from mortgage brokers or direct lenders, giving the servicers fraudulent loans, or loans that were not performing.

At the time, Countrywide Home Loans, which was acquired (in my opinion, it was actually appointed to Bank of America for some reason) was the main lender in the marketplace, the actual company doing the bad loans that caused the market to fail, also became one of the largest servicers, where mortgage companies would sell their loans to Bank of America. Bank of America became one of my main outlets to sell loans to, as they were the last to adapt strict rules and add additional investor overlays, until they got out of the game.

First, let me explain to you what an over lay was, and give you a breakdown of how it worked. An overlay is when an investor is given rules by say FHA, which would say your credit score can't go lower than 640, an investor, in this case Bank of America, would come in and abide by those rules, while Chase, Wells Fargo and Citibank would say even though FHA was at 640 requirement, our over lay is our minimum credit score as a lender is 660. All investors in the market place would make their own rules on top of FHA's rules; usually based on their own portfolio and defaults they were seeing.

When I tell you it was nearly IMPOSSIBLE to keep up with guidelines and take loans, it was. I spent just as much time reading guidelines daily, as I did going out and meeting clients, talking to realtors, and getting business. In addition to credit score

Tip #9

When negotiating your price for the home you are interested in, ask your realtor if the seller is willing to pay your closing costs which is known as a seller concession.

requirements, investors would also make up their own rules and overlays regarding 2,3, and 4 family homes, changing the amount of money needed in the bank, increasing down payment requirements as they felt like it, and also adding in certain amount of established credit card accounts (revolving credit) and consistent employment history without any gaps. Imagine being given rules to operate by, going out and marketing deals and taking deals in, and by time the deal came to fruition, the rules changed, and now you had to restructure everything behind the scenes to still get the deals done. IMPOSSIBLE.

Now, I want to take you on a journey with me, where I give you real life loan scenarios, often time re-structuring deals from other lenders, loan scenarios I faced, and the unfortunate outcome of me being unable to help people get out of loans bad mortgage people put them in. Forget about the business being hard enough as is, it was an emotional roller coaster from every angle. Now, let's take a trip down memory lane.

"Yo Jeff. You gotta meet this guy Mario... here is his number. Give him a call. He's got these condos in the South Bronx and he has been trying to find someone to close the buyer's mortgage for six months now," says J Cruz.

Ring.. Ring.. Ring...

"Hello?"

"Hi this is Jeff VanNote from Jersey Mortgage Compa..."— "Jersey? Why the hell are you calling me?"

"Well J Cruz from REMAX VOYAGE gave me your name and number and said you need help with closing a deal..."

"Yeah, 50 people said they couldn't do the deal. Meet me tomorrow at my attorneys office"

"Ok... well if there's a way to get it done, I will figure it out... I will see you tomorrow"

Now I can't sleep. Another try out! Another challenge to test my skills... one thing I always loved to do was market myself and my company, with desk calendars, planners, handouts, and it just so happened I just purchase really cool LED flash lights... so as a break the ice offering, I gathered 2 flashlights and brought them with me to the meeting.

I showed up just on time at Don Char's legal office... and waited for Mario to get there. Here he comes, happily walking in with a semi smile on his face. We shake hands; he sits down across from me, with his attorney to my left. I handed him the box, knowing the flash light is in the box... he opens it and says "how about I stick this up your ass?" so me, being a 21 year old wise ass, I think I said "how about you stick it up your ass when I close these deals..." we went on to speak of the transactions. Here was the deal scenario.

Mario bought an eight-unit apartment building and converted the building to eight condo units. If the market hadn't crashed, or be in the process of crashing even further, he would have made millions. Instead, he was looking to make his small profit and get out. PROBLEM: Banks weren't lending, and were even more so against lending on condos, let alone NEW condos. His purchaser, now my client, was a 50-year-old Canadian man, who had a boyfriend named Rafael, who was the local drug dealer. He had

> **Tip #10**
>
> Don't lose your favorite home over $10,000. The $10,000 extra in price changes your monthly payment around $50 or so. If you love it, pay for it.

$1,800,000 in a Canadian trust fund, received $7,000 per month from the trust fund in interest, which was guaranteed for life. Awesome right? Well, he had a 590 credit score, paid all of his bills late, and thought I was cute... and, for the record, was very open about it. To make it even better, he would only give me documents I needed in person, at his condo, in the South Bronx. So, one night, I took the trip down to the condo, with my best friend, since a) I didn't want to go to the south Bronx alone, especially at night, and b) I was not too thrilled about his boyfriend being the local drug dealer... so we park out front, illegally, throw the hazards on, and walk in the building, up to the second floor.

Knock knock.

He opens the door dressed like a female, minus the wig. High boots, fake boobs on somehow, and a short skirt... the most disturbing part, he had nude drawings of himself RIGHT IN THE HALLWAY. I swear I couldn't make this up. But, I wanted to prove Mario wrong, and figure out how to get these deals done. So that I did... after two months of speaking with market investors, all of the banks, we figured it out! Citibank, being a local lender, agreed to purchase this loan if we closed this deal. We structured the deal to have our client put $80,000 down on the main unit he was living in, which was his primary residence. The best thing was, he then bought the unit next door, 2a, as an investment unit, with hard money, so he could store his art. We set up the mortgage payment to be automatically deducted the same day as his wire hitting his account from Canada, so the mortgage would be paid and he didn't have to make the payment himself. Just days later, Citibank got out of the correspondent mortgage business and was no longer purchase loans. However, we were able to sell this loan off and close this impossible deal, along with facilitating the private hard money for the other unit, thus closing both deals for Mario. When 50 other lenders said no and couldn't figure out a way, Mario and I did, which led our now 10-plus-years-long friendship, numerous business ventures together and partnerships, and countless life lessons learned. The key to this deal was knowing trust income guidelines, new condo loan guidelines, and credit score requirements along with the down payment needed for low credit scores. Start to finish, it took us 110 days to close this loan, but it was all worth it in the end. I actually wound up buying a unit in this building in April of 2010. I still own this unit today.

"There's no way you can do this deal... I don't believe it"

Bet lunch on it. But first, what's your address? I am coming to your office to meet you in person, and to go over the deal.

"Not your Best Match Real Estate... 123 ABC Road, Bronx"

Great, I'll be there in an hour.

So I show up, November 3, 2008, to a place I have never been before. If you have ever seen the movie *American Gangster*, it is something like that, along White Plains Road in the Bronx. I walk into a nearly empty huge real estate office. I meet with the owner and the realtor, who have both the listing and sale agreement, for $636,000, on a 3 family mixed-use property. The client has about $80,000 in the bank, is in contract, and another lender cannot do the deal. To be clear, the realtor and owner of the company were getting $36,000 in commission if this deal closes... And their lender they currently give business to can't do the deal, because their bank had NO outlet (investors in the secondary market) for FHA mixed-use properties. A mixed-use

> **Tip #11**
>
> Think of a side business to run out of your house so that you can increase your tax benefits by having a home office.

23

property is a property that has residential apartments over commercial space. Since FHA was experiencing the largest losses in the market, due to low credit score and low down payment lending options, they were cutting off lenders in the market. Luckily, since I studied guidelines every day, I knew I still had an outlet left, BANK OF AMERICA. Obviously I didn't tell them my secret, since I learned previously if you share your secrets, or show all of your cards, they can steal the idea or secret and tell another lender, and I was not going to take that chance, but after the deal closed I would be happy to share my secret. So, long story short, I took all of the information that night, called the client on the phone for the entire loan application, and a week later, had the commitment to lend issued. Due to seller issues, the loan didn't close until January 7th, 64 days later. I got the deal done. That day the deal closed, I get a call from the broker/owner of "Not your Best Match Real Estate" saying "Jeff, you did a great job, we want to meet with you to discuss doing future business, this was a great job". I was as happy as could be. I got a very tough deal done, for a great guy, who relocated his church to this building, and even moved upstairs to have his family occupy the building. God was on my side! Talk about rewarding... helping someone not only buy a property, but relocate their business, in this sense, God's house and business, into their dream set up. Talk about live work concept, haha. Anyway, if you couldn't tell, I am a get stuff done NOW type of person, drop everything for my clients and business, and told the broker owner I can meet this afternoon. So, that we did. I drove back up to the now known area, walked in with a big smile, and we set down in a little cubicle meeting area. I was actually expecting a gift, since I saved them a $36,000 commission closed the deal in very quick time frame, and I made about $4,000.... SILLY ME. And just for the record, I am kidding about the gift. My reward was in the satisfaction of closing the deal, and helping my clients, and future referral sources.

So... you'll probably read this in disbelief. The broker/owner asked ME for a referral fee. Yes, you read that correctly. They made $36,000, from my work, my knowledge, my commitment, my training, my brain and deal structuring, and they wanted me to pay them 1% of the loan amount, actually more than I made myself. To take it even further, their actual "proposal" to me was this, "Listen, you did a great job, but here is how this is going to work... we know the bank makes 3 points, or 3% on every deal (A point is equal to 1% of the loan amount, so a $500,000 loan amount, 1 point, would be 1%, or $5,000) so here is what we are going to do, you are going to keep 1 point for yourself, keep 1 point for processing the loan, and we want 1%"... I was in shock. Come to think of it, I actually felt enraged, insulted, and defeated. Everyone thought they knew what was going on behind the scenes at banks, when in reality; all of banks margins got cut. We were lucky to even make 2% on deals, and that is if we were lucky. The market and profit margins changed overnight, and now I had these unappreciative, not respectful men, 30+ years older than me, trying to shake me down, when I just did my job, better than the guys they were giving business to. I will never forget this day, as I can remember it like it was yesterday. I stood up, shook their hands, notified them to call me if and when another deal is in jeopardy, due to their mortgage guy's lack of knowledge, I wouldn't be giving them a penny, and they can have fun with their future... and I walked out. This is just the beginning of what you are about to learn.

It was April 16th, 2009, one month away from finishing my second semester senior year at Fordham. I got a call that night, stating that a deal had to close by the following week, or the client was going to lose $50,000. The

> **Tip #12**
>
> Be realistic with your home inspection. Too many times people ask the seller to make too many repairs and end up losing the deal. As long as the house is safe and structurally sound, move forward.

client had $50,000 at risk in deposit, and their current lender at the time was not getting back to them. That night, I drove to their house in queens and got all of the documents I had requested earlier. I spent all night structuring the loan to meet requirements for FHA. The following day I had the loan committed and approved. The referral source, and clients, were in disbelief. That loan then closed on April 22nd, five days later. The clients had gone to a "low rate lender." Unfortunately due to the mortgage company's underwriters lack of knowledge, they were including debt that they should have excluded, and the clients had to put a few more thousand dollars down to qualify. Once I told them how the deal could get done, they listened and we got the deal done. They were beyond appreciative as we saved them $50,000, and they got their dream house.

This is probably my favorite story. On May 4th 2009, I was walking out of one of my finals for college (yes, believe it or not, I went to this final…) and my phone rang. "YO JVN, I got a friend who just got denied by Quicken Loans. They are saying that FHA can't do deals under 620 credit score any more, is that true?"

"No, definitely not true," I replied. "Actually, we can still do loans down to 580, what's the deal?" "I don't know, call my boy Omar."

Long story short, there were two issues. The first issue is, quicken loans lost their ability to close loans under 620. The second issue was, our client was buying a property that was bank owned, and the FHA appraisal noted the house needed repairs, which in my opinion were complete crap. The repairs requested were for some bathroom mold on the walls to be scraped and painted, and the front steps of the house be fixed, because the brick was broken. So, that night, I drove to this guy Omar's house in the Bronx, went over all of his paperwork with him, made sure the deal qualified based on guidelines. We spent about an hour going over everything. I submitted the loan from his dinner table, and then we got in my car. We drove up to his house he wanted to buy in Rockland County, New York. We looked at the repairs requested, took pictures, and then went to Home Depot to buy supplies. Two hours later, the bricks were fixed and the mold was sprayed, scraped, and painted, alleviating the FHA appraisal issues. We then closed his loan 9, yes 9 calendar days later. We also gave him a rate .5% lower than quicken loans was giving him.

Here is perfect example of creativity of loan structuring. I got a call in early 2010, from one of my college friends. Him and his girlfriend at the time wanted to buy a place in Hoboken. The local lender they were referred to said there was no way to get the deal done, as they didn't have sufficient time on their job, being one just graduated, and one was about to graduate, even though they both had income. I asked if the mother had equity in her home, along with a 401k retirement account. Good news, she did. She was a government worker, and had hundreds of thousands of equity in her home, and a lot in her 401k, so we borrowed a little bit from her home, lowering her rate and payment, as she had a much higher interest rate, so the lowering of the rate combined with the cash out didn't directly impact her pocket, and she borrowed a little extra from the 401k, to use the down payment to help her child purchase a the condo, as their primary residence, with a non-owner occupying co-borrower. Good thing the mom helped, because the condo is now worth $300,000 more than when they originally bought it. I was grateful for them listening to me and having the mother play ball, because at the end of the day, everyone benefited

> **Tip #13**
>
> If your house needs some renovations, always get multiple contractors to price out your requests. Whatever your contractors tell you, add 20% to their estimate to account for any changes.

from it.

There are many other stories like the ones above, and still stories that happen today, in today's market place, where lenders can't do deals. The problem is primarily a lack of knowledge, but also a lack of creativity and thinking outside the box. The key is knowledge on my side, and willingness to listen from the consumer. Together, anything is possible.

Now I want to take you down the opposite road, which is people I couldn't help, because it was too late when they reached out.

In the spring of 2010, banks were experiencing losses from every angle. Quite frankly, in my opinion, this mortgage debacle was completely mishandled. Knowing what I know now, I could have personally implemented rules and regulations for lenders that helped homeowners, rather than hurting them even more. Since the banks, and the higher ups, had never seen such a thing before, in regards to defaults, property values plummeting, along with borrowers being told by lenders to stop making payments, there were people out there that could have had their home and mortgage restructured the proper way, but no, this didn't happen. I had people calling me up who had missed one or two payments, sometimes even by BANK error, and the banks would reject their future payments. Now what does this mean?

Banks are known for trading, selling and buying loan-servicing portfolios. A loan servicing portfolio, to keep it simple, are say 10, 100, 1,000+ loans, bundled up, say 10 loans, $450,000 each loan, totaling $4,500,000 in loans, at 4%. There is a value in having these mortgages, and banks like to bundle up as many as they can, to increase the value, and then sell to another bank. So, if Wells Fargo does 10 loans, they may package those 10 loans in a bundle, and sell them for a nice profit. When they do this, nothing changes for the borrower at all, except where they make their payment. If you were paying Wells Fargo, you may now get a new letter from ABC Loan Company in the mail stating to make your payments to them. Often times, consumers just throw the letter out because they think it is spam or junk mail, when in reality; it is a legal document regarding your loan. Because banks were in total chaos, many loans were being transferred, not once, not twice, but three or four times. Causing significant confusion to clients, especially those set on auto pay, sometimes payments would be taken out and go to the wrong lender, and then the payment would have to be tracked down. It was a complete disaster. So, anyway, let's get into this scenario.

I received a call one day from Joey JuiceBox, who had been living in his two-family home for three years. He bought his house with a no income verification loan, for a very high price, compared to where the market valuations actually were. If I remember correctly, he owed $700,000 and the house was worth $450,000. Owing $250,000 more than the current home value, at an interest rate over 7%, he first called up his bank to see if he could lower his rate, which at the time was somewhere in the 4% range. The person he spoke to said, "Unfortunately, the only way that we can help you is if you miss three mortgage payments."

Meanwhile, the JuiceBox was current on his loan, had an 800 credit score, and never missed a payment on anything in his life. I advised him that if he misses payments, his credit score would drop significantly, and this would cause him to then have to wait even longer to potentially get a new loan, should he want to buy something else in the

> **Tip #14**
>
> Do not pass up a house because the kitchen or bathroom is out dated. Remember, you can always change them to your liking in the future.

future. Against my wishes, Joey went ahead and missed 3 payments. After he missed his third payment, he was given a loan modification package. Since he wasn't familiar with the package, he came to me and asked if I would help him with the paperwork, along with using my fax machine. So, we did. We filled in all of the information, from A-Z, provided all tax returns, house hold bills, bank statements, pay stubs, you name it. 2 weeks later, Juicebox received notification that his loan modification was denied. Naturally, like any other human being, JuiceBox felt duped and lied to. Now, his credit score had plummeted way under 600, he owed nearly $16,000 in past due payments, his taxes and insurance were now in default, and he had late fees for his mortgage. Given the situation, and luckily he saved the money where his payments would have been made. He sent the bank the check for the full amount, including late fees. Good right? Wrong. The check was sent back to him in the mail! That is right. The bank said some bullshit about how, based on their calculations, the only option at this point was a short sale. WHAT? Now JuiceBox is beyond furious. First, they didn't help him lower his payment, then they told him to miss payments and they would help, then they said sorry you are denied we can't help you, then they wouldn't accept his payment, then they said, your only option is to sell your home at a loss!

Now let me explain to you the behind the scenes. Due to the massive amounts of defaults, significantly high unemployment rate, the big banks went on "hiring sprees" and employed people who didn't know what they were doing, and were specifically told to tell people to stop making payments. Millions of people, if not *tens of millions of people*, were getting phone calls and being told to miss their payments. Yes, that is right. You heard it hear. Servicing companies were advising people it wouldn't hurt their credit and they could help, something like a free savings plan, so like your average American seeing an opportunity, don't pay three months payments, save $10,000+,buy a new car, TV, take a vacation whatever, with no repercussion... do so. Well, this went on for at least three more years. This not only impacted people's credit scores, but their future loans to be taken out. At one point, you had to not have missed a mortgage payment for 2 years, to be able to buy a new property and take out a new loan. Today those rules have changed but back then, these innocent people who were misled, were stuck!

So you ask what happened. What did JuiceBox do? Well, JuiceBox decided to move out of the property, buy a nice one family house under his wife's name, move to Westchester County, where they were going to move any way, and he pocketed rents of about $5,000 a month, for nearly 36 months, didn't pay the mortgage, taxes or insurance, and wound up walking away with $180,000 cash, and the property was then short sold for somewhere around $500,000 or so. Given the state of the economy, Obama had passed some rule where borrowers who defaulted and losing their house would not be responsible for the monies the bank lost on the sale. Example, bank lost $250,000 in short sale, borrower at the time had no risk, other than a short sale on the credit report and low credit score. That rule eventually changed and the lost money was taxed as regular income. So, if JuiceBox made $100,000 per year, and the short sale lost the bank $250,000, his income would be $350,000 for that said year.

Now what makes it even worse was, the bank that had the loan had full control. Meaning, if they wanted to sell the property for $300,000 and it was worth $400,000, they would, and then stick the borrower with the loss to pay taxes

> **Tip #15**
>
> Start by purchasing a small condo for yourself. The market will always have a demand for small, affordable living.
>
> **Tip #16**
>
> Condo over Co-Op all day long. Spend a little extra money on a condo rather than settling for a cheap co-op to avoid headaches down the road.

on, according to the new rule. This was just a real messed up time, causing tremendous resentment between borrowers and banks. Talk about guilty by association.

Around the same time I was helping JuiceBox, I received a call from Harry King, who owned a four-family investment property in the Castle Hill section of the Bronx. This is probably one of my craziest stories ever. This client, between his rents of about $7,200 per month, and his 5 parking spots rented out, bringing in $150/each per month, another $750, totaling $9,950 per month in rent, NEVER made a payment. That's right... he never made a payment to the bank. To make it even better, he bought the house in 2006, put no money down, and was making almost $10,000 per month... get this... for 8 years. Finally, in 2014, the bank foreclosed on the property. He made nearly $1,000,000 to himself without ever a penny invested. You may ask how, and why? Well... the bank wound up losing his original mortgage note, and without the paperwork, they couldn't foreclose. Despite the missed payments, the borrower just sat back and collected. In this case, it is clear the borrower took advantage of the system, beat the bank, and walked away with an insane amount of money, but at the end of the day, the banks were exposed for not having their systems in place. This is a very unethical thing to do on the borrowers part, and I don't condone this type of behavior or ethics at all, but this is a very black and white example of just how messed up the times were. Banks were greedy, and sloppy, and this was the outcome, circumstances they had to deal with.

I want to break up this pity party for the time being and interject another wild story. One night, my friend Alex called me up and asked me to come over talk to her parents about their mortgage. Apparently they had received a letter in the mail stating their mortgage balance owed was $0.00, when just 2 years prior, it was

32

about $370,000. As usual, I had never received a call like this, so I chuckled and said I would stop by over that night. This was the fall of 2012. I get to the parents' house expecting to see some BS letter from the lender, and to my disbelief, they were right. Their new mortgage balance was $0.00. It turns out the bank lost all of their loan information, including their original note and mortgage. Since these papers could not be found, the client did not have to pay another penny to the mortgage loan. Let me say this again, the additional $370,000 owed did NOT have to be repaid. The bank, which probably could have been sued somehow, deemed the mortgage balance null and void, and my friend's parents got their house for only 2 years of mortgage payments. Talk about hitting the jackpot. Since I was still in shock, and knew there were scammers out there, I even had the title insurance company run a search the next day, along with my attorney verifying the letter with the lender, all added up. There was NO mortgage attached to the property and my attorney confirmed, the loan balance was eliminated. Now don't get excited, I am sure this will never happen again, but I have heard of other people receiving the same news as I did some research online. This was a crazy, once in a lifetime happening.

My next story brings us to a friend of mine at the time named Louie from Lafayette. Lafayette is a street in the Bronx, off of Tremont Avenue, where Louie lived. Louie was a contractor for 20 years and was great at what he did. When he bought his house, the right way, with a real documented loan, verified income and assets and credit, he was doing for well for himself. In

> **Tip #17**
>
> Always take out a 30 year mortgage on your first property, especially if you plan on keeping the property for a long time and eventually turning it into a rental property or second home. This will lock you into a fixed mortgage payment and you can plan the future around proposed rental income to be received.

fact, he even put 20% as a down payment. Before the market collapsed, he applied for a line of credit, as I believe he bought his house for $250,000, put $50,000 as a down payment, and then the house went up to $500,000, leaving big room for equity to be borrowed. His line of credit had a variable rate, which means his monthly payment changed from month to month. Everything was going great; he bought new tools, equipment, and was even able to renovate his own home. When the market slowed down, his workload dropped off so much that he could not afford to make both payments, along with his workers, and his business suffered significantly. Fortunately, he was one of the lucky ones, able to combine his first mortgage, which was around $200,000, and his line of credit, which was about $100,000, to a new mortgage with one balance of $300,000, at a fixed rate. A fixed rate for a set term, that is. Now, I always recommend clients to consult with both business and real estate attorneys, and I, before signing any documents, however, Louie was embarrassed, and didn't do that. His bank told him he had a fixed rate at 2%. He heard 2% and signed the documents and sent them back, APPROVED. What he didn't read was that yes, his rate was 2%, for the first year, and then would go up, to 3%, then 4%, then to 5%. There was also a clause that stated if he missed one payment, his entire mortgage balance would become due, meaning the entire $300,000, and there would be no forgiving of the loan, and the foreclosure would start immediately. Louie decided to contact me, after he missed his first two payments of his loan modification. Unfortunately, at this point, it was too late. The bank had already begun the necessary filings for foreclosure. Even worse than that, they wouldn't accept his money either. You may ask why in this case? The main reason, the bank knew the house was worth $500,000, and his monies combined owed $300,000, so for them, they could potentially sell the home and make money. There was $200,000 in equity. My Advice to

Louie was to sell the house and take his new money, and buy a new place, either all cash, or rent somewhere for cheap and keep the money in the bank. Eventually Louie sold the house and moved in with a relative, with a little over $100,000 in the bank.

Listen, business is business. If you have a contract or an agreement with someone, or a bank, you are to follow the agreement. The banks though were not doing anything to really help consumers at all. They were simply buying themselves time, or causing borrowers to default, to speed up certain process or acceleration clauses, that would make their lives easier. Many, many, too many people were negatively impacted by situations like above. Right or wrong, people got hurt, by both themselves, and by greedy mortgage lenders.

Consumers will always find a way, and in some cases, they had real creativity. Now remember, I was working for mortgage companies that were experiencing losses on loans at the time, so I was legally obligated to play by the rules, follow the laws, and do things the right way, which I would have done any way regardless, but many people called me with scenarios and schemes you can't even imagine. One guy, whose name I won't even attempt to make up, had three properties. All investment properties in the Bronx. He bought all three properties without telling other lenders, all as primary residences. This is messed up on many different levels, but technology was still not really dominant in the mortgage and real estate game. When the market tanked, he stopped paying all properties mortgages. Despite his occupancy fraud on all of these, occupancy fraud is when you buy a property and say you are going to live

> **Tip #18**
>
> Before you shop for a mortgage rate, make sure you have the house in mind; the lender has all of your paperwork, including a month to date recent credit report. If your lender quotes you a rate without all of the above, you're asking to be lied to.

in it, but never move in, and make it an investment, he chose to short sale all 3 properties to a friend of his that had the cash. Meaning, say he bought each house for $500,000, $500,000 x 3 = $1,500,000... the fair market value was now say $1,050,000, he entered into contract, for all three properties separately, and sold them to his friend, and became the guys partner silently. I tell you sick things went on in the market.

At the end of the day, it was just the taxpayer's dollars that got misused to bail out banks. Banks wrote the losses off, after making trillions and trillions of dollars. Now, knowing what was going on, being in the forefront of the new "norm", which was getting calls from borrowers looking for help and relief, due to them entering into bad loans years prior, I thought it would be smart to short the banks even further, as the public didn't even know what I knew or see what I was seeing. Literally I would say for a good 3 years, 70% of the "Refinance" referrals I received either owed more money on their house than it was worth, lost their job, or were delinquent on their mortgage, behind on payments, and sometimes, all of the above. Back to me shorting the banks, I ended up losing nearly $70,000 in one day. I could not figure out how this was possible... the bank's stock prices were going up, up, and away, yet I was watching people close to me that owned banks, owners that I worked for, taking millions of dollars of losses, and these weren't big banks. These banks were maybe .1% the size of the Wells Fargo, Chase, and Bank of America, if that. Looking back at it, it all makes sense. The people of America got screwed over, lost their homes, lost money by being right on stocks and scenarios, but Wall Street greed wins again. Needless to say, losing $70,000 or so in a day, at the age of 24 was something that made me sick for a long time. The media wasn't helping the case either and everyone seemed to be brushing the serious problems under the rugs.

This next story is really heart breaking. Typically when real estate jams occur, people act out of desperation, and will do anything to get in a deal, and out of a deal. In this case, an 88-year-old woman was federally prosecuted. In 2008, a guy who was friends with someone in the company I was working at wanted to buy two properties. I believe his credit was not sufficient, along with his income. He apparently wanted the properties so bad, that he fraudulently applied for the loans under his mother's name, which was 88 years old. He had her buy both residences, with conventional mortgages, as her primary residence. This all would have been fine, and no one probably would have found out, but he used two different lenders, and each lender sold the loan to the same company, say it was Wells Fargo. When Wells Fargo went to run a social security number check on the borrower, it came up that they purchased another loan the day prior for the same lady, using the same primary resident occupancy. At the end of the day, the son wound up pleading guilty for mortgage fraud and identity theft, and the mother was left unharmed, but this is not something you ever do, especially to an elderly woman.

"Children now love luxury. They have bad manners, contempt for authority, disrespect their elders, and love talking instead of exercise." —FORBES

They Don't Know Anything About Money. According to a 2013 Bank of America/USA Today survey, millennials say they're smart with their cash. They're not. Over half admit they're "living from paycheck to paycheck," according to CNBC.com, and "many are still living with or living off their parents." More than one in three still draw cash or resources

> **Tip #19**
>
> Use a small private local lender with experience. Don't let an online lender cost you your mortgage approval or dream home.

from mom and dad. But one in three are also saving for vacations, and they're saving for vacations rather than homes. But good news: over 80 percent say they'll be richer than their parents.

The above quotes are proof that people have been giving my age group, plus or minus 10 years a bad name for as long as I can first remember hearing the word, Millennial. Having been fully invested and dedicated to my career the last 10 years, I have seen it all, from families collapsing over money issues, homes being foreclosed on, jobs lost, you name it. Collateral damage is a real thing in life, and my belief is that "Millennials" needed to distract themselves from what was actually going on inside the household and in the economy. This is probably the number one reason for the level of entrepreneurship we are seeing today. For a long period of time, there were no jobs available in the marketplace, and more often than not, many parents lost their jobs, which led to kids (Millennials) not having hope, or trust, in finding a job themselves. A Millennial is just a word older people like to pin on us younger generations because they are jealous of the opportunities we are given today, where we can click a button, or post a video, and make money. We can be easy going, work efficiently, and not have to kill ourselves, the ways the older generations did. Work smarter, not harder, is a load of crap. If you work smarter, and you work harder, you are going to be extremely successful.

This book was written to inspire the current age group that ranges from 18-35 years old. As the word "Millennial" gets thrown around lightly, here is the definition according to dictionary.com, "A Millennial is a person reaching young adulthood in the early 21st century."

Individuals in this age range need to know that they do not need the perfect mortgage application credentials to get approved in today's ever-changing real estate and mortgage environment. This book will give you some ideas on what is needed to qualify for a proper mortgage loan, full insight on how to structure your mortgage when applying, creative ways to obtain funds for down payment and closing costs, and when it is best to use certain types of mortgage loans. I want you to take out your first mortgage prior to being 24 years old, just like I did.

The Point is: *You're never too young to invest in real estate, and you're never too young to start studying the Mortgage Playbook.*

According to a **survey conducted by the National Association of Realtors (NAR)**, 74 percent of Millennials think they'll own a home before turning 35. The reasons Millennials are opting out include: mistrust in financial institutions based on what they witnessed during the housing crisis and fear of not qualifying for a mortgage because of student loan debt and a struggling job market. This makes it easier for this generation to be more comfortable living with their parents.

This generational dynamic is a major challenge for the mortgage industry. It's not that Millennials are not as qualified financially or credit-wise; **many are qualified and have the income to afford a mortgage**. There's simply a gap between who's qualified to get a mortgage and who's actually buying.

Tip #20
A creative way to save for a down payment is to contribute $18,000 per year tax free to your 401k and then borrowing the money from it tax free.

CHAPTER 2:

STATE OF THE MARKET

The 2008 Collapse; It will Happen, again.

This time, there won't be a bail out.

There is an old saying that history repeats itself. In this case, I believe it to be true.

Banks take massive losses. They experience a plethora of delinquent loans. They have a knee-jerk reaction and tighten up loan guidelines so essentially no one qualifies.

The Government comes in and over regulates. The market becomes stagnant.

Wall Street realizes they have an opportunity to make a lot of money. Some cowboy creates a new borderline legal loan product.

Banks see the profits and then they do their research. They see new dollar signs and forget the losses they took in the past.

Banks loosen up lending so everyone qualifies again, by dropping credit score requirements, dropping income requirements, lessening down payment requirements. Other banks see what the first banks are doing, and they feel like they are missing out, so…

THEY GET IN THE GAME, too.

In December, 2007, when I accidentally fell into the mortgage business, and by default, real estate, I had no idea about the market, the current lending environment, or really much about business, for that matter. And then, out of nowhere, smack! Right in the mouth. We are in the worst financial and real estate crisis ever seen, comparable to the great depression, some 70-odd years prior. I thought to myself, "What in the world caused this?" "Could people really be that crazy to allow this to happen?" "I have got to figure out a way to prevent this from ever happening again!"

So, I did. I write this today, February 26, 2018, realizing the past 10 years flew by, learning on the whim, seeing crazy real estate stories unfold right before my eyes. Even though I wasn't a part of the cause of the last collapse, I can assure you I will not be involved or associated with the next one. It's happening again. Let me take you on this journey with me, as I unfold where the current smoke is in the market place, who is going to get hurt, and how we can all do our part in avoiding another 2008-style collapse to the best of our ability.

The examples below are just for informational purposes only to help you better follow and read along, and understand what I have seen and my experiences, combined with my thought process and vision of the future.

First, the cost of living has risen so much that anything you buy is over inflated. Look at the price of your cup of coffee, look at the price of your groceries, look at the price of your gas, tolls, heating and electric bill, or even your cell phone or cable bill. I think the cheapest cell phone that actually works, carries about $100 per month bill, or $1,200 per year.

> **Tip #21**
>
> Have realistic expectations when buying a home and let your service providers do what they do best, which is their job. They are the expert, not you, follow their lead.

Cable, $150/month, if you just have basic cable, with maybe a wireless internet and router, that's $1,800/year. In order to pay these bills, you must gross about $5,000, and after taxes, you can afford these bills.

When the market was collapsing, interest rates were between 6.5% and 7.5%, on a regular 30 year fixed rate. Say someone had a $500,000 mortgage, at 7.5%, their monthly payment was $3,496 per month, without taxes and insurances. At the bottom, the 30-year fixed rate dropped down to 3.25%, which if the homeowner with the mortgage was able to refinance, say the same $500,000 loan, $2,176, plus taxes and insurances. Yes, that is right, that is a $1,320 per month savings. Talk about a bail out. Interest rates were reduced by over 50% from the 2006–2007 levels, and many home owners didn't elect to save that difference in savings, but go out and re spend that money, probably on useless items, cars, vacations, dinners, etc. If rates hadn't dropped as much as they did, I believe 8 out of every 10 home owners would have additionally defaulted on their mortgage.

861,664 people lost their homes to foreclosure in 2008. This headline right here tells it all: "Foreclosures up a record 81% in 2008."

If you were a homeowner then, you had four options … Sell and lose money, apply for a loan modification, go into foreclosure, or do a short sale. Because many people had loan amounts higher than what their home was worth, many people decided to do short sales, when there was no penalty to do a short sale, now there is.

Notice I didn't put refinancing on that list? That's right… because no one even spoke of it at banks. Banks (the actual Wells Fargo, Chase, Citibank, Bank of America) were calling consumers and telling them to miss payments. This way, they can modify them and take their loans off their books and deem them a different asset class.

Refinances are now non-existent, at least if the goal is to lower your payment. If you want to tap into your equity and cash out refinance, you can. If you want to go from a 30-year to 15-year mortgage, you can. If you want to refinance someone off your mortgage, you can, but the last 10 years of downward trending, low rates, under 5%, even 4%, is gone, which means, people who accumulate debts, and over spend, are now going to be out of luck. Property values may continuously rise, and I do believe they will, simply from how high rents are and a supply and demand, buyer to house for sale ratio, but the bailout refinance savings are GONE.

If we reverse the example above, from a $2,176 payment to a $3,496 payment, your average American cannot afford that increase. Even if they can, they won't be able to have a Savings Account. Savings in America for elderly generations, people above 70, and younger generations, under 35, are going to be non-existent, or negative, without family help and contributions.

Let's now discuss the cheap money that was borrowed, and the people that left their jobs to become professional house flippers. My Favorite... *not.*

I would venture to say 8 out of 10 house flippers don't have a back up plan or option in the event something goes wrong with one of their flips. In fact, I am very confident that once this market corrects, due to rising interest rates, and people over estimating the upwards trend, 8 out of 10 property flippers either lose everything, or get back to their 9–5 job. There are so many people bidding on properties right now, that naturally, the prices are being inflated. If a good deal

> **Tip #22**
>
> Look at the house you are interested in current tax assessment. If you buy the house for less than the current assessment, you can get the real estate taxes lowered.

on a property is $300,000, someone may buy it for $330,000, just so they can have a new project. House flippers are desperate for deals, because that is their livelihood, that without a deal in the works, they have no future income. All of a sudden everyone is an expert. Everyone got into the game in 2013-14, after the market was stagnant for at least a good five years, and everyone got lucky. Yep, *lucky*. If you made money over the last five years, you were lucky. You weren't smart. The market has rebounded in most areas to higher prices than before 2008 levels. Thank you to low interest rates for allowing this. I will deem those I now consider "Lucky", "Smart" in 7 years from now. If you are still making money, and successfully flipping properties for the next 84 months, then you deserve the credit. When things are good, everyone makes money. When you buy a house today for $400,000, and put $50,000 in it, and the market is up 10% in one year in some areas, you're lucky. If the market stayed flat, you would break even, at best.

Real estate does take some vision and trend spotting, but the real catalyst is cheap money and access to money. If these outlets dry up, and competition becomes overwhelming, which it has been, there aren't enough deals to go around. I had a guy leave his full time job of $120,000 per year, because his cousin made $80,000 on one house flip. It is just insanity. House flipping is NOT a profession, unless you have millions in the bank. House flipping should be a side hustle, side income, family project type of thing, with the right people, for the right deals.

Now the next crash is going to come in the commercial mortgage and commercial real estate field. Many big-time commercial real estate investors borrowed many millions at rates under 4%, and they maxed out their loans. This means, their loan was pushing the legal lending limits with a 4% or under rate. Now that rates have shot up, close to 5%, their loan amount probably will be under water, which means, they need to apply a principal balance payment to their loan, example: you have a $4,000,000 loan, your new max loan is $3.5 million, you need to cut the bank a check for $500,000 to pay down your loan amount. Ok, forget this example, how about the fact that your property is only 60% occupied? You have 5 commercial spaces, and only three tenants. You now have two vacancies... your loan doesn't get the support on paper from your cash flow... unless you have deep pockets, this is an inevitable default.

Rents rose so much that mom and pop companies can't survive and pay rents. Amazon and like companies are putting mid-size companies out of business left and right. Thus, a ghost town. Restaurants are said to make up 85% of commercial spaces over the next few years, well that's great... restaurants also have the highest failure rate out of any business. Now what? Now, the commercial properties drop in value, banks lose money on delinquencies, and no one can afford to even rent the space out at a discount. This means prices drop even further, and further, and further.

Just recently I did the math on the first condo I bought in 2010 in the south Bronx. I am negative $60,000 on it, after vacancies, loss of rents (tenant didn't pay for 6 months) repairs, and gas and tolls to go pick up rent checks. That is right, I lost $60,000 of earned monies since 2010. Luckily, it is a small mortgage amount with a small condo fee, but it doesn't make the $60,000 loss go away. I am confident I will make the money back over time, especially since the south Bronx is booming, and rents are rising rapidly, but if I didn't have a job, and I was just a pure real estate investor, I too would probably have lost my condo or

> **Tip #23**
>
> Don't ever sacrifice service and knowledge for cheaper price. As long as you are getting a competitive rate or charge from your lender or attorney, and you feel comfortable with them as a person, commit.

be in foreclosures. People don't realize that tenants don't pay some times, and vacancies are bound to happen!

I just bought a condo here in Jersey City Heights. I expected it to rent immediately for $1,750. Well, It has been vacant for 2 months now, with a monthly expense of $1,700 including mortgage taxes insurance and HOA fees, and I just rented it for March 1, for $1,595 per month, just to get it rented. Why? Because if I lose another month of rent, I am down another $1,750, so at this point, I need to stop the bleeding. Yes, I will carry a small loss, but $105 per month loss times 12 months, is $1,260, where as one month more vacant is $1,700 negative.

Again, if I didn't have my mortgage income, this would negatively impact me. I luckily have additional income monthly to fall back on, in the event of a vacancy or issue. This is why I also always recommend having 6 months minimum of future payments in the bank for a rainy day fund. Really it should be 12 months for all loans, but you can get away with just 6.

Now, the market may not collapse over night. It may not happen for a few more years. Heck, it may even be 5 years out, but it is going to happen. With new tax law, properties over $850,000, in my opinion are not going to make sense to own any more (residential real estate, condo and one family homes). The high-end luxury market is going to be decimated. The new tax law combined with high property taxes, and interest rates over 5% is a recipe for high-end disaster.

On the bright side, my belief is that you should buy ANY real estate under $250,000. Even up to $400,000, I believe you will be safe. As long as your total monthly payment is under $2,000, with taxes and insurances, you will be less likely to get hurt, as everyone in America can use affordable living, and especially an affordable monthly housing payment. I believe we are going to see a BOOM nationwide in any real estate under $250,000.

Fake Loans are back! Now, this is where I get passionate. The same types of loans that took down the market 10 years ago, are back, and are in full force. Now, remember, I was not in the game then! But, I am now, and I can tell you first hand, CONSUMERS CALL UP ASKING FOR 1) STATING INCOME LOANS, 2) NO DOCUMENT LOANS 3) HARD MONEY LOANS and 4) LOANS THAT DON'T NEED TAX RETURNS or CREDIT REPORTS.

The psychology behind this… You have loan officers that need to feed their families or pay their bills. You have lenders (banks) harassing loan officers to send them these types of loans, and you have consumers calling and asking for the loans.

The result is why I am no longer doing residential mortgages. Yes, I still motivate and inspire and help my team of loan officers who I have spent the last few years training, but I am in no way shape or form originating these loans. People who do not qualify on paper for loans should not be able to get loans, especially on housing! If we make money easy to get, this artificially inflates prices to levels they shouldn't be. Real estate values should rise and fall organically, based on the market, and based on supply and demand, NOT based on someone who won a lawsuit for $200,000, and wants to buy a $600,000 piece of real estate, and put $180,000 as a down payment with no income. It is just bonkers to me how this is happening again.

> **Tip #24**
>
> Always make sure you have money set aside that you don't touch, for a rainy day, emergency fund, for your home. I recommend having 6 months of mortgage payments set aside.

Wall Street gets greedy—Banks get greedy—Loan officers get harassed—Consumers get greedy and desperate, and BOOM! 2008 all over again.

There are scary times ahead, especially for the individual and small real estate guy. Those with deep pockets can weather any storm, and I am not worried about their future. I am worried about that single mother that can't afford her house any more, I am worried about the kids that see mom and dad going through a divorce over finances, and I am most concerned about that elderly man or woman that is losing their home because they simply can't afford to feed themselves and keep their roof over their head.

CHAPTER 3:

MILLENNIAL CLIENT REVIEWS

Rachel Sandora
Senior Vice President Client Relations at Nationwide Property and
Appraisal Services LLC
May 25, 2015, Rachel was a client of Jeff's

Many loan officers get a tough reputation for being "salesman" instead of facilitators and not really caring about the borrowers themselves, but more about the deal. Jeff could not possibly be farther from that. He was recommended to me via coworker and within 2 minutes of the first phone call – I felt totally assured. He asked me for all the info he needed, wrote and sent my preapproval letter and told me to have fun seeing homes.

As a young woman working in the mortgage industry myself, I thought I had a pretty good understanding of the process and what it entailed; for me, my agent, the sellers, etc. And then.... I fell in love with a home that was for short sale. For anyone that knows anything about them – one they aren't short and second, they can be a miserable process. Thankfully – I had Jeff and Jersey Mortgage at my side.

Anything the short sale bank needed from Jeff or his team was provided same day or next day at latest. While

> **Tip #25**
>
> Always get a realtor to represent you. I don't recommend going direct to the seller as some times disagreements happen and you need that middle person to keep both parties happy and calm.

the same cannot be said for the short sale bank – he has the quickest response I have ever seen. You would think I was the only client Jeff had at that time due to the attention he provided. He made sure I understood what I was signing and after ever package sent to me – believe me I had questions! ☺

The entire process took almost 10 months. While the wait and uncertainty were miserable, Jeff and JMC were a dream to work with. Even my realtor was impressed and commented multiple times throughout the process how happy he was to have Jeff on the back end.

I would highly recommend his services and honestly could not say enough great things about him. I have officially been a homeowner for 5 whole days now!!!! New and exciting things ahead and I have Jeff to thank.

Vancestone Hall
IT director at Peter Thomas Roth Clinical Skin Care
June 10, 2012, Vancestone was a client of Jeff's

I was only allowed to choose 3 attributes for Jeff but if I could I would choose them all. He is a man of his word, he lays it out all the details and gives you all the information you need before you need it. If I ever need to buy another house I will be sure to seek him out.

We weren't ready, but Jeff got us there

cmjagger from Maplewood, NJ, March 27, 2017

My wife and I weren't planning to buy a house, at least not for a couple of years, and definitely not until we were good and ready. We were just exploring and trying to imagine life with our three kids outside of New York City, killing time on a day off from work. Turns out, life in the town looked good, better than we could have thought, and we stumbled upon an adorable house that we couldn't walk away from. At our realtor's urging, we gave Jeff a call. From the start, he was friendly and comforting, perfect for two people who had no idea what they were thinking. But more important, it was clear he knows the business inside and out and he had solid answers to even our most ridiculous and I questions. Then, after we got our preapproval and won the bid, started getting our financials and paperwork in order, paralyzing fear set in. But Jeff, a natural educator, was on hand to reassure me every step of the way, answering text messages within minutes, no matter how early in the morning or late at night. I think it's safe to say anyone who's gone through the process of obtaining a mortgage knows it can be a nerve-racking (even shattering) process, but Jeff's hand-holding approach and his attention to detail left me feeling taken care of. What's more, from the time we made our first call to Jeff, his predictions seemed to differ from those of his peers and from what was being predicted in the news. Of course, the market is anyone's ball game...but Jeff's predictions are the ones that came true. We got our mortgage without a hitch, and that adorable house is ours, thanks to him and his team (big shout-out to Iris). Three weeks after closing, I got a text from Jeff, just checking in, asking how life as a homeowner is. I'm hard at work trying to get friends and loved ones to move to our new town, and you can be damn sure I'll be sharing Jeff's info with them when the times comes.

> **Tip #26**
>
> Have all of your paperwork ready prior to even talking to a lender. Be prepared.
>
> **Tip #27**
>
> Try buying a home in the off markets... September to March, usually you get a better deal and it is less competitive as people like buying in the spring and summer.

Saved the day

kreedo7 from New York, NY

I was approved for a loan with another major bank. However, the property was not approvable. At the last week before closing, the bank notified me that I could not get the loan. I was ready to give up but my realtor contacted JMC and advised Jeff about the situation. Jeff took on my application and found a way to get the loan and at a .50% point cheaper than what the other lender was offering and about .25% point that my existing loan. THANK YOU to Jeff and the staff at JMC for saving the day because I was convinced nothing more could have been done to get a loan for my property.

Jmc team is a godsend.

Cdanielloislandwide from New York, NY

"I started realizing paying rent was only helping the person who owns the house pay their mortgage, I reached out to a friend who recently purchased a house with Jeff and his team at JMC. I called Jeff the same day and two days later he came to my apt and sat down with me and my family explaining everything we needed and showing us how possible it was for us to be homeowners. My credit score was not great but he told me it was possible, while looking for a home and simply because of pure stupidity I let my credit score drop dramatically. Jeff worked with me and helped me go from a 525 credit score to almost a 650 in less then a year, even saving me $8000.00 at closing because my credit score was over 640. It seemed like the hardest part was over, I was wrong. Paper work is probably the most stressful part of the whole process, getting all the papers needed to prove you are ready seemed like it would never end and then Rebekah walked into my life. Rebekah basically held my hand with all the paperwork and documents I needed, countless mornings she would call and help me and explain it all to me. I was prob not the easiest client being that I'm not good with computers and was always working when they needed something but Jeff and Rebekah got it done for me. I really owe a lot to these two awesome people and highly recommend Jeff, Rebekah and everyone else on their team at JMC. Being in my own home is one of the best feelings I've ever had and I owe it all to Jeff and his team. I highly recommend them!"

Jeff was a God-send when I first bought my home 6 years ago...who else could I turn to when I wanted to refinance!!!

Zuser20160405121253970 from New York, NY

6 years ago I was introduced to Jeff. I was a nervous first time homebuyer who needed all the help she could get...and Jeff gave it to me. He dealt with me honestly and calmed my fears with his knowledge of the "business". He told me exact what I needed to do and he took care of the rest.

When I saw the market change and knew I could refinance, I spoke with many different banks and brokers, but I could not trust what they where saying to me---I did not feel they had my best interests in mind. So I went looking for Jeff ☺ Glad I did!!!!! Again, Jeff told me what I had to do and he took care of everything else. I have recommended him to my friends and I highly recommend him for anyone who is looking to get their first mortgage or refinance.

DREAM TEAM — First time homebuyer with an amazing experience

> **Tip #28**
>
> Sacrifice your current wants and needs to start building up your credit and savings so you're able to easily purchase the real estate of your dreams.

n general from Hoboken, NJ

If you are reading this review, you have found the right team for your lending needs. Jeff, Rebekah and his team at JMC are amazing. Jeff was recommended through a friend and it was the best decision I have ever made. Being a first time homebuyer, there are a lot of questions through the process and Jeff was there for us. You can tell Jeff has been in the business for a long time and answered all of our questions while giving us sound financially advice. He helped us tailor our loan to fit our needs and really helped alleviate anxiety during a stressful process. I will be recommending Jeff and his team to everyone I know looking to buy a home. Thanks again Jeff for helping us with our first home purchase!

I knew that any referral a family member would give me had to be a good one, but...

zuser20140223125758771 from Teaneck, NJ

I was referred to Jersey Mortgage Company, specifically Jeff VanNote and Rebekah Tardieu, through my Realtor, who is also a family member. I knew that any referral a family member would give me had to be a good one, but Jeff, Rebekah and the JMC Team surpassed even those expectations. They walked me through each step of the mortgage process, answered all of my questions and provided me with the assurances I required as someone who didn't have a completely perfect background. Best of all, I learned that they are not here to judge you, but are really here to help you, which couldn't have been more appreciated. Please do yourself a favor next time you're looking for a mortgage/refinance and reach out to true professionals—Jeff, Rebekah and the JMC Team. You will not be disappointed.

Once, in the middle of a dinner and totally unrelated to his business with us...

jmelendez409 from New York, NY

Not having an "American nuclear family" Jeff understood and was able to meet our needs. Once, in the middle of a dinner and totally unrelated to his business with us, we called to ask for his opinion of an issue we were having, He pulled himself away from his dinner companions and gave us his full attention. He is hands on and genuinely cares for his clients.

I would recommend him to everyone, no doubt!! My husband and I call him our "...

user36538242 from Oceanside, NY

It's a known fact how applying for a mortgage could get very stressful. Not with Jeff, from the very start he was very accommodating with all our questions and explained everything to us that we understand every little thing. This is my second time buying a property but with so many new laws and new rules I still felt like I was confused.... Not to mention was also scared. Jeff was very patient with the whole process and he guided us from the beginning till the end. Everything was done right and that's how we knew we were in great hands with Jeff. I would recommend him to everyone, no doubt!! My husband and I call him our "Angel" since he was like that to us. His guidance and patience with us was unremarkable. He treated us like family and nowhere can you find that in this crazy world of business. Jeff, thanks so much for everything. We will be forever grateful for your kind heart.

> **Tip #29**
>
> Rates are still low, if you can get a rate under 5%, you are lucky!

HE IS A TRUE MAN OF HIS WORD which is almost impossible to find in this or any business.

Daviddiaz7214

My wife and I are in the process of buying our first home. Jeff has been a pleasure and true asset to work with. He has guided my wife step by step through the process of buying a home, which for a 1ST time homebuyer can be very stressful and confusing. HE IS A TRUE MAN OF HIS WORD which is almost impossible to find in this or any business. And his quick responsiveness, and recommendations to other professionals in the home purchasing experience has EXCEEDED our expectations.

He also connected us to a lot of great people who helped us even further with our...

LaLaLauren from New York, NJ

My 56 partners and I were very nervous going into buying our first home. Jeff was great in guiding us through all the details of a home buying process. He also connected us to a lot of great people who helped us even further with our house purchase.

When 99% of the people in his industry walk away after a closing never to be heard...

56nnmarie skelos from Rockville Centre, NY

I'm not one to write reviews or critique other people's performance but when an individual goes FAR above and beyond what is expected I have to take notice. I work in the real estate industry and I've dealt with hundreds if not thousands of Mortgage Brokers / Bankers. Believe me when I say this, this man is the best. Not just because he is competitive or knowledgeable or efficient with getting the customer exactly what they want. He is the best at what he does because he cares more about the people he deals with than he does about anything else. He asks the questions others won't ask to make you feel comfortable with making one of the biggest financial decisions anyone will probably make in their life. When 99% of the people in his industry walk away after a closing never to be heard from again, Jeff takes the time to follow up with his customers not because he has to or someone told him to but because I just the kind of guy he is. I have 10 years working in the industry and there is only 1 person I would ever recommend to anyone I like or care about I buying or refinancing a home.... Jeff VanNote

He made us feel comfortable and understood how stressful the process of purchasing...

sdivito from New York, NY

Jeff answered all of our questions as honest and best as possible. He would even respond to text messages at all hours of the day. He made us feel comfortable and understood how stressful the process of purchasing a home could be. He promises to help us with future refinancing and any other issues.

Jeff hustles hard and is super smart when it comes to getting a deal across the...

gakinnagbe from New York, NY

Jeff hustles hard and is super smart when it comes to getting a deal across the line which is a lot better than the big banks have done for me. He helped me buy my first home and came through

> **Tip #30**
>
> Keep renting if you are comfortbale... but start planning. Always have the option available to you to purchase a home.

where others couldn't.

Jeff was easily accessible and responsive to all questions.

User4060300 from Weehawken, NJ

It was a pleasure to work with Jeff and the staff at Jersey Mortgage. Jeff was easily accessible and responsive to all questions. Clifton Savings Bank gave my girlfriend and I an issue over our work history since we had just graduated from college within the past 2 years. Jeff gave us no issue with this and helped us buy our first home. Thanks Jeff!

Jeff made that happen.

Elisabeth44 from New York, NY

For several years, I had approached my bank about refinancing my property when the interest rates dramatically dropped. Yet, the bank had consistently turned me down—although I had strong assets, great credit, and other strong criteria for refinance. Then, I was recommended to Jeff Van Note. In contrast to the corporate bank, Jeff provided me with a clear outline of my qualifications, and offered me a clear path to refinancing, guiding me through a systematic process, along with support and optimism. One and a half years ago, Jeff's financing helped me purchase my family's new home. Once I bought our current home in 2013, Jeff then promised to help me refinance (although he had already secured an extremely low interest rate for the initial purchase)—and he did so this month! In the end, he helped me purchase a townhouse, which I had dreamed of, and then help me save me thousands of dollars by refinancing. His company also assisted me with significantly reducing the closing costs, which was extremely generous. I only wish I had known of Jeff's company years earlier so I could learn of other options than having to deal with a cold, disinterested corporate bank and not lost tens of thousands of dollars to them. Jeff made that happen. Clearly, he is superb at his job, very dedicated and conscientious. I give him the highest ratings.

Jeff showed up after his workout in his gym gear ☺ and we discussed my loan requirements ...

abhishek89c from Jersey City, NJ

At the outset, it's my first review for anything, ever...I was recommended to Jersey Mortgage Comp (and Jeff) by my realtor, told that they have a streamlined and smooth loaning process. As always, I had my doubts but I had few earlier experiences (with listed banks) to relate/compare with and put things in perspective. After the initial phone conversations with Jeff, I got a " we'll make it work for you " vibe, followed by a meeting where he came over to discuss my loan requirements. Jeff showed up after his work out in his gym gear and we discussed my loan requirements, he gave me very straight forward answers(not that he'll check and get back) on what can/cannot be done. Also advised me on my options and the best way forward. After the handshake I knew it would be done and indeed , it was done as we closed yesterday (he left, not before predicting a Mayweather win!) I would use them again simply because they are very professional and its an in house loaning process, decision makers, underwriters all in-house, So the turnaround time is very less...and you get answers right away and not get tied up in banking bureaucracy.

Tip #31
Always inspect the boiler and hot water heater. Most last 7-10 years.

Jeff also provided great guidance when we hit a bump in the road.

Shannonpwales from New York, NY

Jeff no words can describe his patience and understanding. From the beginning of the process he provided us with great responsiveness. He told us every document we would need before we go get the process moving and kept us informed along the way. Jeff also provided great guidance when we hit a bump in the road. There was not a day throughout this long ordeal that he did not send an email or text update letting us I know what was happening. In addition, his knowledge regarding finance was phenomenal.

He never disappoints, always has sound advice and is very involved throughout the...

user96744949

Jeff VanNote is fantastic! I rarely write reviews, but Jeff is the type of professional who deserves nothing but top reviews. My husband and I have worked with Jeff several times over the past 3 years (on a home purchase, a re-fi, and a construction loan). He never disappoints, always has sound advice and is very involved throughout the entire process to ensure your best interests are protected. He's also got a great network of other professionals he works with from attorneys to credit fixers. He's going to make sure you come out on top!—Kelli

Jeff came through and saved me when I was in the process of closing on a condo purchase...

user14339023 from New York, NY

Jeff came through and saved me when I was in the process of closing on a condo purchase, my original lender had declined my financing on a technicality at the last moment. He was very solid with approving & processing me.

Unfortunately, Jeff was not the first mortgage professional involved in my deal.

Christopher Duran from New York, NY

I could not have been more pleased with the service and expertise provided by Jeff. Unfortunately, Jeff was not the first mortgage professional involved in my deal. The original guy dropped the ball and was not able to secure a loan for the property, putting the deal in jeopardy. Then Jeff came along with an excellent loan product, a speedy approval, and brought us to closing quicker than we thought possible. We can't thank him or recommend him highly enough!

Has a professional and diligent work ethic; he has expert opinions on market trends...

user76670900 from Jersey City, NJ

I've known Jeff since April 2011 and he has been a pleasure doing business with him thus far. He first assisted me with a refinance for a property in NYC. That process went smoothly without a hitch considering this was during the 2008-09 credit crisis.

Most recently Jeff assisted with my purchase of another property in Jersey City. In this process all the mortgage brokers I shopped around with were adamant the purchase could not be done without less than a 20% down payment. Jeff proved them wrong and produced a package that suited my needs to a successful purchase!

Jeff has a professional and diligent work ethic; he has expert opinions on market

> **Tip #32**
>
> Look to acquire 3 properties in the next 10 years. One property to live in and two investments. By time you are ready to retire, you'll have a nice monthly income.

trends in the real estate industry; and is always available to provide insightful advice. He listens to my concerns, does not force his opinion and has consistently followed through on his commitments.

As things moved along with the house, I paid for an inspection and the bank ordered...

dcollogero from South Toms River, NJ

From the first hello Jeff VanNote gave me back my peace of mind and was able to trust another mortgage co. I had a terrible experience with my mortgage lender. I trusted them since I had my current mortgage with a company I knew, or thought I knew. I filed all my paper work with the mortgage co and paid for a filing fee. Once the mortgage processor received and went over all of my paper work I received an e-mail to start looking for a house. Before I started giving any of my paper work to the processor I also told my processor that I did a modification on my current home a year ago in order to be able to keep my home and my processor replied "no problem." I also faxed over all the paper work for the modification at his request. In the meantime, I found a house and went into contract. Once all the paper work was in order by the processor it went to the Underwriter for review and stayed with the underwriter for 3 weeks. In the mean time I was asked to explain why I did a modification by letter. As things moved along with the house, I paid for an inspection and the bank ordered an appraisal, so you would think everything was moving along smoothly. After the appraisal was done I received a phone call from my processor and also another processor asking questions concerning my modification date it was a three-way call. Both processors wanted to know the date of my modification and I said it is on the papers, well it went silent for a minute and they both said they'd have to call me back. I received a call by both processors half an hour later to inform me that I could not have the loan since I did the modification a year ago. Nothing was told to me in the beginning of the process when I told my processor regarding the modification. I had already left my job and I was just devastated and just lost for words, but then I came out and said to my processor if you knew I could not have the loan then why did this even go to underwriting or even pay for filing fees etc. His response to me was I'm so sorry this was completely my fault I did not check the date. In using Jersey Mortgage Co. there was no stress at all my processor was on top of everything and I had no stress at all, what a difference. I recommend this company to anyone who is looking for people who are helpful and caring, and that's what you will find with Jersey Mortgage Co starting from hello.

Jeff was this someone for us.

Vishavjit from New York, NY

Jeff knows how to get things done no matter the challenges. He works with you as a team member to serve all your mortgage needs. He helped us purchase our first home. It was a long slog and you need someone with knowledge, patience and the wherewithal to circumvent all the trials and tribulations of this life altering process. Jeff was this someone for us. We are working with him on the refinancing of our mortgage knowing without a doubt he will make this happen as well. We highly recommend Jeff.

This step was crucial and I am grateful Jeff was willing to meet me several times...

jpsmittal from New York, NY

> **Tip #33**
>
> Take your annual income and multiply it by 30% Write that number down. Now take your annual income and subtract your annual rent. Write that number down and multiply that number by 30%. If there is a $2,000 difference, you need to buy a home!

It was a pleasure working with Jeff to get my home purchase financed. I started working with Jeff several months before I started my home search and he helped me narrow my focus and understand what all my financing options were. This step was crucial and I am grateful Jeff was willing to meet me several times before there was any deal on the table. Once I identified a property and got into contract, things moved extremely quickly and I received a commitment within 2 weeks. There were a few issues with the property itself, but these were resolved and in the end we had to convert the loan to a 203K, which was again handled by Jeff in a seamless manner.

What most impressed me about the way Jeff works: Immediate response, every time I texted or emailed Jeff I received a response within a few minutes. Extremely Knowledgeable and gives you a realistic assessment of what your options are, will not over-promise to win your business.

I would gladly use Jeff's services again, and in fact look forward to working with him again in the future.

Zillow Hurt the Game; they didn't change the game the way I thought they could.

The game really changed when Zillow entered the marketplace. I was actually the first paid advertiser in the Harlem market, which is still Manhattan, but was severely underpriced as at the time, not many savvy realtors were marketing to this demographic. I strictly did this paid advertising because my realtor referral source asked me to, and I believed it was a strong and cost efficient way to brand myself in an untapped market. I believed in Zillow so much so that I put a lot of money into it, as you can see by the trade confirmation below.

7/20 ZILLOW INC.

PURCHASE 1,500 SHARES @ 34.3198

$51,555.05

I soon realized that the word was out on the street about Zillow and realtors and lenders flocked to this "new" way to work, by purchasing monthly advertising on this site. I spent anywhere from $300 to $2,000 per month spread out over a few different markets, the Bronx, Harlem, and a few towns in New Jersey, only because my realtors wanted me to be their preferred lender. The best feature on Zillow turned out to be the Zillow Lender Profile, where you can get client reviews. In 2016 I stopped all of my paid advertising on Zillow and wound up getting more leads based off of my free lender profile, than I ever got with my paid advertising. As Zillow began to grow market share, consumers, and by consumers I mean future homeowners, current homeowners, and realtors began complaining. The way Zillow visually shows their pay to play realtors (realtors that spend the most amount of money) on listings is deceiving to people searching for properties. The people searching for properties would call the top recommended realtor, who appeared to be the realtor to contact for the listing for sale, and that realtor wouldn't ever get back to the consumer, or not be able to contact the actual listing agent. Consumers were then left hanging with no answers. As the listing agent, they had the exclusive right to represent their listing, and their contact information was all the way on the bottom of the site, in very small print, where unless you know this, you would never even scroll down far enough to catch this information. Now, the biggest problem of them all was the

---

Tip #34

Respect your realtor's time. You never have to pay them, as the seller pays their commission. Commit to them if they are working hard for you!

---

new Zillow "Zestimate." Zestimate is defined as Zillow's estimate of the home value. Great, Zillow should have checked their algorithm and accuracy first before launching this "zestimate" which inevitably gave consumers false hope as to what their property was worth, and made it much more difficult for honest realtors to get listings for actual market value. I can't tell you how many past clients called me and would say "well Zillow says my home is worth…" and then we would get an appraisal, and it would be off by over $100,000, + or -. Meaning, if Zillow said the house was worth $500,000, the appraisal would come in at $600,000, which is an actual federal valuation, or $400,000 valuation. After so many calls, I decided to look into how this discrepancy. Zillow was pulling data from homes in a zip code, not making adjustments for updated homes or out dated homes, condos or co ops, one, two, three, or four family dwellings. They were simply going based off of price per square footage, which is not the way real estate is valued. If you have a 4,000 square foot one family home, and a 4,000 square foot three family home, they are not the same value, they can be in rare cases, but not often seen. What really set me over the top was the day I bought my most recent flip, at 694 Bloomfield Avenue in Nutley NJ. I bought the house for $188,000, and the house was a complete wreck. It needed about $80,000 worth of work to make it livable. The day I bought it, my Zestimate said it was worth over $450,000. If I was a consumer in the market and had no idea about real estate or values, I would think "Wow, I can get a $450,000 house for $250,000, what a deal!"

I didn't like the fact that consumers were being deceived and sellers were being harmed as Zillow's Zestimates even caused home sellers to sell their property for less than market value due to consumers seeing this zestimate number. I wound up selling my 694 Bloomfield house for $375,000, all fixed up, which was still way off from their high "Zestimate."

In order to create awareness, at one point I created F*CK ZILLOW summer tank tops. I didn't do this to hurt Zillow, and to be honest I don't even care about Zillow, I did this to grow consumer awareness. People were getting hurt and to make a statement, I made this shirt and wore it often. I even got messages from realtors around the country that I sent these shirts to, and I gained heavy support. Zillow's platform is clearly all money driven. They get realtors and lenders to pay crazy monthly fees, and deceive the consumer, oh yeah, and make great realtors lose opportunity because new realtors want to over pay for ad placement.

CHAPTER 4:

INCOME – HOW DO I KNOW?

Income, credit, and assets, OH MY! Don't be alarmed. You can't fault yourself for High school or College not teaching you how to qualify for mortgage loans or purchase real estate, which most likely at some point in life, you will be doing both. As you read this book, I want you to realize just how easy it is to get a mortgage, with the proper guidance and support of course. I want you to get excited and think about your dream home, or place to live, with the happiest of environments and settings you can image. Why? Because you have earned that right. Haven't you heard of the American Dream? The American dream has always been home ownership, and thanks to the government creating and allowing low down payment option mortgage programs, you can achieve this dream potentially sooner than you have imagined.

Let's first take a look at the word INCOME. What is income? Income is considered to be money received, especially on a regular basis, for work or through investments. Now if you are reading this book, investments may not apply, however, if you are fortunate enough to already have investments, then we will lay out some great options for you as you read along. The key words in the definition of income are regular basis. Mortgage Lenders aka banks define regular basis income as someone who has been on the same salaried position, at the same company, for a minimum of 2 years consistently, with no gaps and no breaks. It is believed that if someone is to stay on their job for that time period, their income is stable and very likely to continue. Now if you haven't been on your job for 2 years, or aren't even in the work force yet, don't panic, there are ways to get a mortgage in just 6 months. Let's look at types of income banks use in order to qualify you for a mortgage loan.

W-2 Income – W-2 income is when you receive pay stubs, weekly, bi-weekly, or monthly, that usually more often than not, add up to the same amount each time frame, and sometimes include overtime, bonuses, or commissions. In order for W-2 Income to be used and considered for qualification purposes, you must be active on this current job.

Here is an example of what would NOT work to qualify as income:

Sideline Steve worked from June of 2015, to October of 2017, making an annual salary of $60,000 per year working for Bill's Discount Furniture store. After discussing with his wife, he decided to pursue a new passion of snow shoveling, since the winter was rapidly approaching. He decided to open up his own LLC called "SIDELINE STEVE SNOW SHOVELING LLC", and wants to buy a house.

It's now February 2018, and Steve got his W2 in the mail, showing his earnings. He also just made $10,000 from December 1st to January 31st in his new LLC.

Here are the FACTS:

Steve cannot use his prior employment as income to qualify for a new mortgage, because he no longer works there. It doesn't matter Steve's credit score, it doesn't matter how much money Steve has. For his new business, he cannot use that income either, as a self-employed borrower must have 2 years of

Tip #35
Group chat everyone in your family. Suggest buying a vacation home where everyone chips in. Everyone loves vacations.

established business, documented by tax returns with income properly claimed and filed.

What are Steve's Alternatives? Think outside the Box.

1099 Income & Business Income

Ok, so you're self-employed. We get it. You have a lot of income and also have a lot of expenses, along with a creative accountant. In order to use 1099 income and/or business income, you must have two proper years of tax filings. This means that you have to file 2017 tax returns and show money made, and then show 2018 tax returns with money made. Here is the catch, if you made LESS money in 2018, than you did in 2017, for whatever reason, you can only use the 2018 income, due to what is called declining income. Declining income is when you make less money in the most recent year, opposed to the prior year.

Let's take a look. Silly Cesar made $50,000 in 2016 flipping and trading cars. Technically, he made $4,166 per month, or $50,000 divided by 12. Now in 2017, Silly Cesar turned up the volume, doubled his revenue, but bought 10 more cars, and only claimed $36,000 in income on his tax returns, which is $3,000 per month. If applying for a mortgage loan, the bank will only give Cesar credit for $3,000 per month in income, even though he made purchases of additional vehicles, his net income is what is used to qualify.

Now let's flip the scenario. Silly Cesar decided to go all in for 2016, and made $10,000 net profit to himself and filed it on his tax returns. Great year! Now, for 2017, he is all profit and made $100,000 in filed tax return income. Here is how the bank calculates silly Cesar's income.

2016 - $10,000; 2017 - $100,000; $10,000 + $100,000 = $110,000; $110,000 divided by 24 months = $4,583.33

So, what should silly Cesar do? THINK!

Fixed Income such as Social Security, Disability & Pension

Now, this makes sense. Dino the Dinosaur just retired from flipping flapjacks at Malibu Diner. Why did he retire? His wife Harriet just got her pension from the schools and his social security check just kicked in. Dino was on temporary disability for flipping the flapjack too high in the air and burned his nose, having him receive a settlement from Malibu Diner for $100,000. Wow, what a flip! Since Social security and Pension are guaranteed for life, the day these both go into effect, they can be used to qualify as income. An awards letter must be provided and accepted, and receipt of payment must be proven. The $100,000 settlement cannot be used as income, but can however be used for a down payment on the brand new luxury townhome Dino and Harriet want to buy.

Trust Income

I hope you are reading this and are lucky enough to have a trust. If you do, you will *love* what you are about to read. As long as the trust shows you getting a guaranteed amount for the next 36 months, the bank will use that income for you to qualify for a mortgage. They will also give you credit for a portion of the balance in the trust account to show as assets, or money in your name. The money must be guaranteed to a set amount and the trust docs must be provided to be reviewed by the lender in order to properly calculate your qualified income amount.

> **Tip #36**
>
> Don't wait for the perfect property. Buy the property in the perfect location, and make the property perfect for you.

Interest Income

In order to use interest income from stocks or dividends, you must have two years of tax returns filed with the amounts. Just like above for the 1099 & Business Income, the monies must remain the same and/or increase over time to be used properly. If you are liquidating a stock or bond, or investment account, the interest cannot be used as you are no longer maintaining that balance in the account.

CHAPTER 5:
CREDIT – IMPORTANCE
OF YOUR SCORE

I owe you. You owe me. We are one big happy family.

Credit is a very important tool in the real estate world, and in life. Credit bridges the gap between what you need now and can't afford to pay in full, or bridges you from one situation to the next. It is recommended that you always take your credit and payments towards your credit seriously.

Many banks require a credit score of 700 to get a loan. Some banks are requiring 660, others 640, a few 620, and even less at 580. Banks are allowed to make their own requirements for minimum credit scores for housing loans. Certain mortgage loans require certain minimum credit scores. I personally recommend being over 640 before applying for a mortgage, but in the event you are not, it is okay, there is a chance you can still do your mortgage approval down to a 580 credit score, but the guidelines will be tightened to qualify and your loan application will be heavily scrutinized.

Here are some great ways to establish credit at an early age, even before applying for a mortgage or having a job/career.

Tip #37

Reading book doesn't make you ready to buy a home. Putting your trust in professionals makes it easier to be ready to buy a home.

---

1) Always ask mom or dad, or brother or sister, to be added as an authorized user on their credit card. You will get credit for their excellent payment history. Always get added to a credit card that maintains a low balance and is paid every month, on time. Please note: If the person who adds you misses a payment, you will have your credit negatively impacted.

2) If you are 18, go to your local bank, and apply for a secured credit card. You can't get turned down, unless you have bad credit already in some instances. In this event, you give Big Bad Bank $500, and they give you a credit line of your own money for $500, and you manage it accordingly. Be sure to keep low balances on the limits so you don't over extend yourself.

3) Try and put a car loan in your name and make payment history. This will show banks you are able to make a same monthly payment, every month, on time. Even if you split the payment with a relative, who cares, as long as you are having it reported to your credit.

The best advice I can give you or anyone else is to make sure you always pay your minimum payment before 30 days are up. You do not want a negative remark on your credit report, you do not want any late payments showing, and you definitely don't want to be delinquent on any debts at time of application for any new line of credit.

Credit scores are important, however, things happen and I understand it all. I have been doing this too long to realize people are people, humans are humans, and we all make mistakes. It is best to get your credit checked every 6 months or so, with a full tri-merge credit report rum by a lender to get an accurate score report for you. Credit reports range from $15-$40, depending on what information is provided on the report.

CHAPTER 6:

TIPS FROM THE BETTER QUALIFIED

1) Get Credit – Use it

Too many times, people get credit cards and use them once or twice. They then never use them again. The credit card companies end up closing the card out for non-use or lack of activity. When this happens, you lose all of the history on that credit card. By no means do we say to over use your credit, or by things you cannot afford. We simply suggest to use your card every month, maybe a few times, to buy small things. You can even pay off your card every month in full, so long as you use it. Even though you are paying off your card in full, you still get credit for having a balance and using it frequently. Eventually, the credit card company will raise your limits allowed and this will help increase your overall credit profile as well.

2) Do NOT co-sign for anyone

Many people are going to ask you in life to help them. We encourage you to help people, but we do not recommend you co-signing for anyone. Unless you are fully prepared to make someone's entire monthly payment, simply put, just don't do it. Your credit score can only be negatively impacted by co-signing for an installment loan, which is a mortgage or car loan, and that means that you have all the risk and zero reward.

Recently I received a call from a friend of mine who is a realtor. Prior to him calling me, I received a text "need a magician, call me" – usually when I get a text like this, it means I have to get creativity and think outside the box. When I spoke with my friend Eric, he said his 77-year-old client went to another bank, despite him referring him to me. After three weeks of having his client's loan in process, their loan was denied due to a foreclosure that came up. The client's credit report did not reflect any foreclosure or delinquent loan. When the bank ran their fraud guard, a property came up from 2015 that had been foreclosed on. When the elderly man was asked about the address, he said it was his daughter's and he originally was on the mortgage loan, but was refinanced off of the loan. This was partially true. While he was refinanced off of the loan, for some reason he remained on the deed. When the foreclosure went through, even though the loan was not in his name, the property itself was foreclosed on, and now he would have to wait 7 years to get a new loan. The good news is, we were able to get him a reverse mortgage on a purchase mortgage loan to have him buy the house, but if this program didn't exist, he would have been all out of options. It is very important to know and read all of the documents and ask all relative questions, as the past can come back to bite you if you don't know what you have gotten yourself into.

Tip #38

Use your tax refund for your down payment!

Tip #39

You can't borrow your down payment monies. You can only get a gift or use your own funds.

3) **Don't use cash**

There is no history or track record of cash. It doesn't help you in the future. It may help you budget, but in our opinion, one day there will be no cash in the economy. It may be 20 years from now, but as you can see already with digital currencies, Venmo, Zelle, Quickpay, no direct monies will be changing hands. Get used to budgeting and spending within your means.

4) Care about your credit and check it

There are many free credit report options. While the scores aren't always accurate, what is on the reports usually are. I recommend doing a life lock, which locks your credit and notifies you every time your credit is pulled or someone tries to use one of your credit cards. It is something that you should take pride in, and not be worried about, but monitor accordingly.

5) Don't max out your credit cards

We all want to buy nice things, but when you max out your credit cards, your score suffers tremendously. When you have high balances to your limits, usually anything over a 50 percent balance, drops your score monthly. If you have multiple cards over 50 percent balances, your score will plummet 20,30,40 or maybe even more points. If you have to max out a credit card, before you do it open up two or three other credit cards and spread the balance out over those cards to eliminate the high credit usage.

6) Don't close out credit card accounts

So what if your credit card rate goes to 18%, don't keep a balance. Problem solved. The only time I recommend closing a credit card account is if it has a fee. If not, keep your cards open. Your longest open cards are the best ones for you to keep open forever. When you use them over time, with a tremendous credit history, the bureaus like this and your score keeps going up, up and away. If you use a card for 20 years, and then close it out, it is almost like you never even had it in the first place. Get rewarded for your hard work and credit history—don't erase it by closing it out.

7) 92% of car insurance companies check your credit

While I don't agree with this at all, credit should have nothing to do with auto insurance. I get their logic, but that is like saying someone who is a terrible driver should have higher interest rates on their credit cards. Since this is a policy of many car insurance companies, you want to keep your credit score as high as possible. These insurance companies are all about risk. Risk risk risk, and that is it. They look for ways to raise your premiums and justify charging you more money year over year. This is probably their number one way of doing so, without you being in an accident or having a bad driving record.

8) 50% of employers check job candidates' credit

Again, I don't agree with this practice either, but it is true. One out of every two employers checks your credit. Many people just view someone based on their credit score. A credit score in my opinion is not indicative of someone or their ability to repay. You can have a 650 credit score and never missed a payment on anything in

> **Tip #40**
>
> Ask your lender if they can pay all of your closing costs. If you get a higher interest rate, there is a chance they can!

your life. It is absolutely absurd and ridiculous, but if employers do it, even more the reason to have pride in your score, monitor it properly, and follow the tips to boost your rating.

Real Estate under $500,000; Why Buy?

The truth behind Affordable Real Estate

You're probably thinking $500,000 is way out of your budget. And it may be. It is for many people surrounding the NYC area. However, with the way rents are currently increasing, you are better off taking the plunge now, than waiting another 18 months.

Let's talk payments real quick. If you are spending $3,000/month, you can afford a $500,000 home / mortgage. Taking the average interest rate of 4.125% on a 30 year fixed rate, your monthly payment is $2,423 per month. In your first year, of that first 12 payments (12 x $2,423 =$29,076) $20,464 is interest, which is fully tax deductible. We will get into the tax savings down below in this article but lets stick to the payment for now. So, $2,423 for your mortgage, lets just estimate $300 per month for PMI (Mortgage Insurance) (if you do not put 20% down OR if you do not buy out your PMI) estimated real estate taxes annually $7,200 per year, or $600/month, and finally home insurance, let's call it $100/month.

Mortgage—$2,423
PMI—$300
Taxes—$600
Home Insurance—$100
Total new payment—$3,423 per month

Did you know that 100 percent of your interest paid is tax deductible? Well if you didn't, that is ok! Because it is. So what does it mean? Let's use an easy example for informational purposes only.

If you make $100,000 per year, and are in a 30% tax bracket, you pay $30,000 per year in taxes. If you make $100,000, but spend $20,464 in that year on mortgage interest, your new taxable income is $79,536, and 30% of that $23,860.80 in taxes paid.

What does it all mean?

It means, by having a mortgage of $500,000, in your first year alone, you will have saved $6,139.20 in income taxes paid. If you divide that number by 12 months, you're keeping an additional $511.60 in your monthly paycheck! Or, depending on your tax with holdings, you may just get a larger tax refund by the $6,139.20 at the end of the year. Please remember the example above is just an example and you need to consult with a knowledgeable accountant to tell you your specific tax benefits of home ownership.

If you are paying rent for $3,000 per month, and decide you want to buy a home, and take out a $500,000 mortgage, after your tax deduction, you're actually saving money. $3,423-$511.60=$2,911.40.

Your home can also be utilized as your savings/investment account. As you pay your mortgage monthly, you pay down your loan amount. It is absolutely the best thing one can do in their lifetime. Create wealth with your home!

Tip #41
Ask your landlord if they are willing to sell you their property. Avoid having to move.

Make the sacrifice and investment of home ownership for your family. You owe it to them!

CHAPTER 7:
DETAILS OF THE MARKET

ASSETS—IS THIS AN ASSET?

We are going to start off by playing a game. I am going to name something below, and you decide if it is or is not an asset in regards to a mortgage application... Ready, Set... PLAY.

Your college degree

Your diamond earrings

Your leased car

Your purchased boat

Your checking account

Your cash value life insurance policy

Your personality

Your smile

Your grandmother's savings account

Your security deposit where you are currently renting

Ok... Let's see how you did.

Tip #42

Get a financial accountability partner to be transparent with and motivate each other to save, pay off debt, and improve your credit

---

No

Yes

No

Yes

Yes

Yes

No, sorry!

No, sorry! Although it may get you a better interest rate!

YES – if you are the beneficiary or your name is on the account, OR, if she is on your application

Yes… a security deposit can be used as an asset

Assets, for the most part, are just used to confirm where the down payment is coming from for you, along with if any additional cash reserves are required from you to have in the bank at closing to make sure you can make your payments and have a cushion for financial security. However, once closing is done, you can do whatever you want with the monies you have. I do usually list all vehicles, jewelry, accessories, and life insurance cash values, to show the bank you have items that could be sold or traded in the event of a financial hardship. This again is not necessary. I usually recommend showing the bank you have the down payment, the closing costs, 3-6 months of payments set aside to have in case of an emergency, and life insurance, especially if someone is married and the spouse is not on the loan, so the bank sees an additional risk reducer.

DOWN PAYMENT—HOW LOW CAN YOU GO?

Twenty percent down or LESS? Less. Always. If you take a look at the time value of money, money is cheap, and investment returns, such as the stock market are high. I am going to break down the past 10 year recent trends that I have seen, and these can change on a daily basis, and my mentality can shift drastically based on new news or events, however, I stand by this opinion of you putting less down and keeping more money in the bank.

Let's take a $400,000 one family house for an example.

If you put a $14,000 down payment, and have a $386,000 loan amount, your principal and interest monthly, over a 30 year fixed rate term, at a rate of 4%, would give you 360 payments of $1,843.

Now, if you make a 20% down payment, with a loan amount of $320,000, over a 30 year fixed rate term, at a rate of 4%, you would have 360 payments at $1,528.

Let's compare. The difference monthly is $315. The difference annually is $3,780. The difference over 30 years is $113,400. Now the good news is, your either going to refinance or sell your home in 5 years, just like every other American. Now, don't forget the difference of down payment, which is $66,000 ($386,000 - $320,000). The average return on investment over time in the stock market is 7%. So if you take that $66,000, and return on average 7% annually, and have borrowed money at 4%, locked in and fixed for 30 years, in 30 years, that $66,000 would be worth $502,409. WOW. The numbers make sense if you choose to look at them this way. This applies only when rates are

Tip #43
You are never going to be 100% ready to buy a home. Just do it…

this low in the marketplace. If rates creep up over 5%, the numbers would not be as attractive.

BUT WHAT ABOUT PMI? —R-E-L-A-X

PMI. Who cares? Not me. I took out two loans with PMI. The first one in, April of 2010, was an FHA loan, and it is because I only had about $15,000 for a down payment, and I didn't care, because I wanted to buy the property. I would much rather pay a higher monthly payment, rather then laying out 20%. The good news is, on conventional deals where you get PMI, once you have the property for 2 years, and the property goes up in value to a certain amount, you can request it be removed. 9 out of 10 times, in an appreciating market place, I am able to get my clients PMI removed after 4 years of paying your mortgage on time. How? Combine the paying down of the initial loan balance, with home prices rising consistently, the gap between the value and your loan widens, and the risk becomes much less. In some cases, we can do a refinance where we can restructure your mortgage, and you are able to buy out the private mortgage insurance.

What exactly is PMI you may ask? Well, PMI is another dumb insurance product that allows insurance companies to make unnecessary money. PMI is private mortgage insurance. Mortgage insurance comes with a lot of unknowns, but let me break it down for you so you can understand it as best as possible.

Say you are buying a $400,000 piece of real estate. If you put 20% down with a conventional loan, you don't have to pay PMI. Now if you put 10% down, or anything less than 20% down, you will pay PMI. If you put 10% down, or $40,000, and take out a loan amount of $360,000, the lender implements PMI, and orders PMI for you, and you pay an insurance for the difference between your loan, and the 80% loan to value, in this case you are paying PMI on the $40,000 difference between $360,000 and $320,000. PMI payment is calculated based on many factors which include but are not limited to type of real estate, 1 family, condo, 2 family, your credit score, if you are buying a home with someone else, the lowest middle credit score of either of you, your debt to income ratio, your loan size, and the state in which your property is in. To keep it simple, the higher the credit score, the more you put down, the lower your debt to income ratio, the cheaper your monthly mortgage insurance will be.

As an example, if you have a $360,000 loan amount, your annual PMI factor may be .25%, or $900/year, which is $75 per month. Now, depending on the type of loan that you take out, and whether it is Fannie Mae or Freddie mac, you may have PMI for a minimum 2 years. These rules change over time and usually never in the borrowers favor.

Let me give you an example I personally went through. In 2016 when I bought my condo, I paid $350,000 for it, and I put 10% down, and had a $315,000 Fannie Mae loan. A year later, I had my condo appraised at $440,000. Great. Well, kinda. I was always told as long as your loan is 78% or less of the appraised value, your PMI would come off. I spent two months researching and submitting requests to have the PMI removed. It was over $200 per month extra I was paying. Finally, I got an email from some supervisor stating that I had to be at a 70% loan to value AND pay PMI for a minimum for 2 years. This was insane and obviously I wasn't happy, but the rules are the rules.

If I wanted to get out of my PMI, I would have to go through a refinance,

> **Tip #44**
>
> Walk around your neighborhood and see what is for sale. See what is available and at what price point.

spend thousands of dollars on closing costs, reset my mortgage, and at the time, rates were higher than the rate I had. So, I decided to wait out for another 12 months, pay the extra $200 per month, which is $2,400 extra, and then reapply in July of 2018.

So back to what PMI actually is, is it insures lenders against losses, who take on loans higher than the 80% loan to value. So the PMI company only has risk on the small difference of the portion of the loan amount. They are only insuring the lender against the $40,000 in the case stated above, and are collecting basically free money. According to an article I read, less than 1% of all PMI loans actually default.

Unfortunately it is the necessary evil in this case. I would rather avoid putting 20% down, keep my money in my pocket, and pay the extra insurance premium. Especially in an appreciating or increasing market, when values go up, it is easy to refinance out of PMI loans, or simply just wait the 2 years and have the sufficient equity needed to apply for removal.

WHAT IF I WANT TO BUY AN INVESTMENT PROPERTY FIRST? YES!

I love this idea, and in an expensive market, like the New York and New Jersey Real Estate market, it sometimes makes more sense to rent, and buy a cheap condo somewhere down south. I always tell younger kids to buy their retirement home now, or their favorite vacation home now, so by time 10 years flies by, they are already making money on their investments and don't have to worry to scramble, or feel late to the party. I definitely recommend speaking to an accountant about tax implications for you, based on your income, salary, assets, and see where you can get the most bang for your buck tax wise, along with a few real estate markets that may be up and coming, so you can buy real estate low, and sit back and watch it grow as you get older.

WHERE I WENT WRONG—SHOULDA, COULDA, WOULDA

I elected to use my FHA loan on a condo as my first property purchase, rather than a multi-family home. If I had guidance, or if anyone knew anything, they would have told me, Buy a 4 family for $450,000, put down a little under $20,000, live in one unit, and rent the other 3 out. But, no one likes to see other people succeed. So, no one told me that. However, I tell everyone that. If you are able to use your FHA loan, which allows you to put just 3.5% of the purchase price as the down payment, you can be the first time home buyer, and have 3 renters paying your mortgage and in some instances, putting money in your pocket monthly as additional income, thus, you living RENT and MORTGAGE free. You are able to use your FHA loan for any 1,2,3 or 4 family home, and sometimes on a condo, if the condo is approved for FHA. Most are not approved. This will allow you to be hands on, as an owner, as a landlord, and receive a ton of tax benefits. It is very important to work with a local professional realtor to work for you, and get you what you are looking for, which meets all the requirements you have. The numbers don't lie, and if the numbers make sense, then the numbers make CENTS, and do the deal!

The unspoken truths of mortgage lending and top 10 suggestions on picking a lender

Everyone is only concerned about interest rate. 99% of the time my initial conversation and interaction with a client starts with "What's your rate" or "My bank is offering X%, you need to

> **Tip #45**
>
> Buy out your PMI on a conventional loan with less than 20% down.

be lower than that to get my business"... and the sad thing is consumers will always find an answer they want to hear. Now that mortgages are getting easier again, and it doesn't take a rocket scientist to structure financing, and the computer does a good portion of the work, first day in the business want to be loan officers are fielding calls, or "leads" and misleading and misguiding consumers in the wrong direction. At the end of the day, the industry has become flooded with people with no experience, no knowledge, and no ethics, causing it nearly impossible to do business and make a living.

If I were a consumer shopping for a mortgage loan, knowing what I know now, from having closed over 1,000 clients, I would look for the following and do these exact steps.

1) I would never shop online. You're giving your information to a complete stranger, over an APP, or through a server, and the likeliness of being hacked is very good.

2) You don't know who is handling your paperwork.

3) You're probably never going to meet the person who does your loan.

4) Face to face interaction and shaking hands will always be the best business practice, especially when dealing with everything from your social security card, to your bank statements, to your tax returns.

5) I would always ask a family member, a realtor, my accountant, or my financial advisor for a recommendation, or I would ask someone who is invested in real estate to refer me to their guy, so that I know I am in good hands and have someone to hold accountable.

6) I would use a mortgage banker, who can lend money direct. Mortgage bankers who lend money direct control the entire process start to finish and don't have corporate non-sense to deal with. Mortgage bankers only stay in business by originating and closing mortgage loans, so they have an incentive to approve and close your loan as quickly as possible.

7) Choose someone that understands what you're going through, guides you and tells you the truth, not what you want to hear.

8) Let the professional do their job. Move at their pace, not your own pace. A lot goes on behind the scenes that you will never know about, so have patience and trust the process.

9) Never pay origination fees, including application, processing, underwriting or commitment fees.

10) Pay points if you want a lower rate, run a break-even analysis and see if it makes sense to do so.

Mortgages and real estate will always be a relationship business. Some people will always go online, shop until they drop for the best rate, but it does not turn out to be productive. When the market turns and things go wrong, the market will lose 90%+ of its loan officers that just got in the game to make a quick buck and then they are on to the next business. The mortgage business is the least transparent process and business in the country to my knowledge, and there are

> **Tip #46**
>
> Always change your lock when you move.
>
> **Tip #47**
>
> Buying a home is easy. Maintaining a home is difficult.

too many people that factor into the experience. Too many people have to do their job for things to best work out.

CHAPTER 8:

MY DOG SAID... I SAY SHUT UP!

Understand that everyone is raised differently, has different perspective, and truly looks at life from a different place. What I can tell you is, do what works for you. At the end of the day, if you want to buy a condo, buy a condo. If you want a two-family home, buy the two-family home. People are going to try and protect you and give you all sides of the outcomes, but at the end of the day, you have nothing to lose. Take the risk, do what you want to do, and buy real estate. There has never been a better time than now, and as time goes on, rates will go up as will prices, and you will be paying much more in the long run for waiting on the sidelines. Knowing the facts, having the right team behind you, compiling data and seeing trends will all be great, but like NIKE says "JUST DO IT".

Shopping for interest rates is like driving around looking for gas stations each day for the lowest prices, only to find out some gas stations advertise credit prices, and some advertise gas prices, and some gas stations don't show the price including tax. There are something like 50,000 lenders in the United States. By time you find a lender that works for you, someone else has a lower rate. If you want to get the best rate, you have false expectations and won't ever be satisfied. There is true value in having a loan officer or lender that gets your deal closed, assists when issues arise, and gets you a fair competitive market rate. Just like any other profession, what you

> **Tip #48**
>
> Don't pay your rent in cash. Always document your proof you pay on time.

pay for, is what you get. If you want a great doctor and your life is on the line, are you going to say give me the cheapest one? No, you are going to want the best. If you are in a lawsuit, you are not going to hopefully select the guy that charges you $100 an hour, but the guy that maybe charges $250 or $300/hour. Price is certainly what you pay, but value is what you get.

When people first call me or start a conversation and the first thing they say is what is your rate? I immediately tell them I think they should call up other lenders and I don't think their priorities are straight. A great loan officer is so much more than a rate. There is so much behind the scenes that goes into a mortgage, from unlimited pre-approvals, credit checks and evaluations, structuring of loans, hand holding a client from start to finish, and then after, under appraisal situations, monitoring interest rates, knowing loan programs, knowing tax implications, and truly advising someone on a large financial decision, in most cases, the largest they will ever make. I myself can never find the lowest price, and quite frankly, I don't always want the lowest price in anything. I want and look for a fair price. Every lender has rates within .12% or .25% of one another. Shop service and track record and professionalism.

Make sure you do not shop rates until you have all of your documents in line, allow a lender to pull your credit, and have a property in contract. Shopping for rates prior to finding a property is like buying a crib for a baby when you don't even have a boyfriend or girlfriend yet. Follow the necessary steps so you can maintain your sanity and peace of mind. If you do this, I assure you that you will be happier, much more calm, and understanding. Do not get caught up with rates. Get caught up in the excitement and bigger picture! Home ownership, or refinanced mortgage.

Banker Vs. Broker

There are many benefits to working with a banker, and there are also many benefits to working with a broker. The best is a hybrid, which is a direct lending mortgage banker, with the ability to broker. Not many are both, but the ones who are typically close a lot of deals and have a ton of market share.

A direct lending mortgage banker has the ability to disclose your loan, set your loan terms based on the market, and control the process from application to funding/closing of your loan. They don't need to wait on third parties for processing or underwriting or closing, and this is the absolute most seamless process. With that said, some bankers are limited on deals they can close, and also have limited capital in most cases. They can only do certain deals, and underwrite to a specific set of guidelines.

A mortgage broker has zero control, usually works for a fee paid by the borrower, or sometimes even the lender, where the lender gives a higher rate, and pays the broker a fee for sending them the deal. Mortgage brokers were big in causing the market collapse, and for a while, mortgage brokers became extinct. Mortgage brokers usually don't have any risk or skin in the game, and therefore structure riskier loans. The benefit is, a good broker can find you a great rate with a lender that actually can close your loan. The negative is, they have no control over the process or time frame, and can't ask underwriters or closers for favors or rushes, in the event they are needed.

Now a hybrid is the way to go. I would only deal with a banker that has the ability to broker. This means they have access to the best rates, all of the mortgage programs in the market place, and control the entire process. This

> **Tip #49**
>
> Check the ceilings and walls for leaks or fresh paint jobs that may be covering up old water spots.

assures me I am getting the best rate and the best service, in efficient time frames. I know they are working directly for me, and have my best interest in mind. I have taken out numerous loans and have always used a direct mortgage lender with the ability to broker, and I always will.

CHAPTER 9:

CREATIVE WAYS TO SAVE AND GET MONEY FOR A HOME

Trying to figure out how you'll start saving up to buy a home? Here are 13 creative ways that I promise you will work:

1) Have your parents give you a gift—there are no tax implications under a certain amount but please consult with an accountant prior

2) Have your grandparents give you a gift – there are no tax implications under a certain amount but please consult with an accountant prior

3) Block your federal and state with holdings from your paycheck, so rather than you getting a tax refund at the end of the year, your accountant can advise how many dependents you can have so that you don't owe money, and you are not getting any refund either, and you are getting more money back per pay check

4) Sell some old items and keep the receipts to track

5) Find a friend with money and buy the property with him or her. Work out an agreement where your income and credit is used, along with his or her monies,

> **Tip #50**
>
> Check "DOM" or days on market on a property listed for sale. Find out why the house hasn't sold if over 30 DOM.

income and credit.

6) Live at home or with friends to save up.

7) Get a part time job

8) Collect cans and bring them to recycling centers

9) See if your town or state have any down payment assistance programs to help you

10) Ask your parents to take out a small mortgage to help you

11) Ask your parents to take out a line of credit to help you

12) Contribute $18,000 to your 401k over the course of the year and then borrow the monies for a down payment, all tax free

13) Side Hustle doing something that interests you—Uber, eBay, whatever

There many different loan types in the marketplace. The key is to find the right real estate. Once you find the right real estate, the proper loan can be figured out. I recommend going with an FHA loan or a regular conventional mortgage, depending on what type of property you are buying. Some properties have restrictions to loan types, down payment amounts, credit scores, and other variable factors.

How to find a Deal in Real Estate

I'll show you what to look for. Everyone and their mother is now a real estate investor, property flipper, and know it all… Because they have gotten lucky on an upward real estate market trend. I started my career in the worst real estate market and lending environment, back in December of 2007, when the last bubble burst and home owners were years in default, getting foreclosed on, and real estate speculation was at an all time high.

I am going to walk you through my step-by-step process on what I look for in a deal, and how I am patient in new markets and investing my money, but when I finally do, I go all in.

I recently closed on a condo in Jersey City Heights, 75 Palisade Avenue, Unit 1. It is a 600-square foot condo, with a private deeded backyard. This means I have exclusive access to the backyard.

First, let's start off how I found this. My realtor has me on auto notification any time a property is listed. My mindset, after lending in the area, and living in the area since 2014, has been to buy anything under a $400 price per square foot, with an ask price under $250,000, along Palisade Avenue. I got an email saying this property had a price drop and I put an offer in for $210,000. It was accepted. I then wired a $42,000 good faith deposit to hold the deal, while my mortgage application was being submitted and approved by my bank. So, it is VERY important to work with a LOCAL real estate professional who not only knows the business, but knows how to put deals together.

Location, Location, Location!

Journal Square PATH train...A .6 Mile walk... 10 minutes or less if you are mildly in shape.

It's 2.8 mile walk (if you take the longest route possible), more like a 1.2 mile walk if you cut through side streets, to the HOBOKEN PATH train.

> **Tip #51**
>
> Always ask the seller how much their current heating and electric bill is to build this into your budget.

A direct line to the Holland Tunnel, which is probably 4/10s of a mile from the condo, via a direct shot.

Finally, a 5.6 mile walk / drive to Times Square, which 4.5 miles of that is going up Palisade Ave, down into Hoboken, over to Weehawken, and through the Lincoln Tunnel...

So the first thing I look for is the LOCATION and the proximity to public transportation. WHY? Public Transportation means people who work can get around, and can pay more rent, because usually they do not have a car. With this location, you can access two path trains, take the bus, or even drive your car and be in NYC in less than 5 minutes if you drive yourself.

The second thing I look for is, Does the rent I can receive cover my mortgage payment? If so, I buy it. WHY? What about return on investment? Well... In this area, the rents are still low compared to Hoboken Rents. The same apartment in Hoboken would rent for $2,500 per month, whereas this apartment will rent for about $1,800 per month... so as time goes on, my rent will go up and my mortgage balance will be paid down! Free easy money, tax free (hopefully).

The third thing I look for is buying at a discount. This unit, at time of acquisition, was appraised at $250,000. The price per square foot I bought it at was $350, and now the going price per square foot is now $500 Approx., which now values the condo unit at about $290,000 or more. Not a bad deal.

Also—I paid my real estate lawyer in Bitcoin.

The final thing I look for, and one of the main factors in buying residential real estate is the ability to have upside, or value increase over time. I believe this area, which already is proven by the above paragraph, showed signs of massive appreciation. I believe this area will one day call for a $750-$800 price per square foot on certain real estate pieces, due to the over flow from Hoboken, and our belief that Jersey City Heights is the Next Brooklyn... which I encourage you to check out our site www.THENEXTBK.COM—which we own and operate.

SO, this is a quick and easy success story, purely based on 3+ years of fact finding, trend analysis, and pure supply and demand in the market place, all backed by a decade long career of mortgage lending, starting in the Bronx, and beginning lending in Brooklyn back in 2010, where I saw similar trends.

CHAPTER 10:

REAL ESTATE...
PARTY OF...A LOT!

Here is a full list of people involved in your home buying experience. This list could have more, and it also could not include some parties, but here is who is involved.

1) YOU

   Your main role is to locate the property you want to purchase. You have the final say, no one else. Pick your teammates and service providers carefully, then release control, and trust the process.

2) YOUR REALTOR

   Your realtor is to negotiate the price and terms and deadlines for you. They are also supposed to give you good solid referral sources from attorneys, to lenders, to insurance providers, to handy men, plumbers, electricians and guide you on a tour of the   neighborhood so you learn the local eateries, places to go, and where not to go, if they exist.

3) THE SELLER'S REALTOR

   The seller's realtor is to let the appraiser in to inspect the property for valuation, along with letting the home inspector in to make sure he or she is making reasonable requests. They are also make sure the time line is moving as planned according to the contract. Their main focus is to make sure the property sells for the highest and best price with   most acceptable terms for the seller, their client.

4) YOUR ATTORNEY

Your attorney's main function is to protect you. Your attorney will review the terms and guidelines and add in or remove clauses to make sure you have limited to no risk, and if something goes wrong, they are able to get you out of the deal. They are also responsible for reviewing title insurance and making sure there are no liens or violations,   or unpaid judgments against you.

5) THE SELLER'S ATTORNEY

The seller's attorney does for them what your attorney does for you. the sellers attorney is to clear title as well for his or her seller and make sure the loan payoff is in, if the seller has a mortgage on the property.

6) A TITLE INSURANCE COMPANY

A title insurance company is to do all research against you, the seller, and the property. Title insurance 99% of the time is ordered by your attorney or your lender. This is a very important piece to the transaction, and is there to protect you.

Tip #52

Find out if your real estate taxes include school tax.

Tip #53

Everyone wants a deal. Don't over negotiate.

7) A SETTLEMENT COMPANY

A title company is also known as a settlement company in some states. A settlement company gets the money from the bank or lender and disperses the money to the appropriate parties.

8) A BANK ATTORNEY

New York requires an attorney for the lender. The attorney for the lender re-clears title, reviews and drafts all documents, and makes sure the lender is protected and all Ts are crossed and I's are dotted. The borrower is responsible for a bank attorney's fee.

9) A LOAN OFFICER

A loan officer's main function is to quarterback you and your loan through the process. He or she structures your loan, advises what programs you qualify for, works with his or her operations team, and locks in your loan when necessary.

10) A LOAN OFFICER ASSISTANT

Usually this person, if they exist, is your day-to-day contact who handles your paperwork. They work very closely with the processing and underwriting team and make sure your loan is buttoned up and ready to get closed as quickly and efficiently as possible.

11) A PROCESSOR

A processor is the one who processes the paperwork you provide. They review bank statements, verify deposits, review pay stubs and verify employment, and order 4506-t forms which verify with the IRS your tax returns are paid. Essentially a processor is the one to package and present your loan for approval to the underwriter.

12) AN UNDERWRITER

An underwriter is the one who actually approves your loan. Different underwriters have different capabilities of approving different types of loans. Underwriters use their own discretion to approve or deny loans based on their experience and federal loan guidelines.

13) A CLOSER

A closer is one who receives final insurances and taxes and drafts closing documents with correct dates, and finalizes all closing costs. The closer is the last stop on your journey to closing. A closer works with the title and settlement companies, along with the attorneys to get the loan and deal closed.

14) A HOME INSPECTOR

A home inspector is to point out hazardous or structural property defects. They are also good at locating mold or maybe even

---

Tip #54

The only income that matters is your current income. Your old income or "maybe getting a bonus" does not matter.

---

termites. From my experience, too many inspectors over inspect properties. No property is perfect. Be careful of what you try and negotiate following your home inspection. You are best to let your realtor negotiate for credits or repairs.

15) AN APPRAISER

An appraiser's main job is to create an opinion of value based on recent comparable sales of like properties. This means it is an opinion, not a fact, based on a physical inspection. An appraiser's job is to give accurate information, and a local appraisal company is best to use, since areas change from block to block and street to street.

16) AN ENGINEER

An engineer usually only is needed when there are thought to be structural damages, or if you are doing a construction loan and are changing the property. If you are building or renovating, you may need an engineer.

17) A SELLER(S)

A seller needs to hire a realtor and an attorney, and sit back and relax. I recommend them starting to pack when they go into contract. They should look to move about a week or so before closing, this way the house is empty by time of closing.

18) A HOME INSURANCE PROFESSIONAL

A home insurance company or broker is to properly insure your property against theft and unexpected events. I personally think everyone should use a broker for home insurance, and not the company you have your auto insurance with, as often times you can get a much better price on home insurance when someone shops your quote for you.

19) A TRUST AND ESTATES ATTORNEY

Typically a trust and estates attorney is brought in once your net worth is over $1 million. However, if you need a good will, or need your deed changed for whatever reason, seek out someone who is not overly expensive. The more assets and net worth you have, the better counsel you should seek out.

20) A FINANCIAL ADVISOR

Your financial advisor does not know mortgages. They also don't know what is going on in the mortgage market behind the scenes. They do know money, and they do manage your investments. Financial advisors are good if you need a plan or have a goal to save a certain amount for retirement. Oftentimes they access your investment accounts and send over to the bank your statements of assets.

21) AN ACCOUNTANT or CPA

Once you own real estate, you need a CPA. You need someone other than HR Block or any other tax preparer. Real Estate and Real Estate tax implications are complicated. Spend the extra money so you can maximize your tax refund and avoid paying unnecessary

> **Tip #55**
>
> Pick out your house. Get a contract of sale. Then worry about interest rates.

taxes.

22) THE IRS

The IRS makes some rules in lending and has to verify your taxes are current. If the government is down, typically the IRS is down, and they have delayed, antiquated systems in place.

23) THE FEDERAL HOUSING ADMINISTRATION

The FHA is a mortgage insurance company, insuring lenders for mortgage loans to borrowers typically with riskier loans, higher debt ratios, lesser credit scores, right now down to 500, and low down payment options.

24) FREDDIE MAC, FANNIE MAE

Freddie and Fannie are loan servicers that make the rules for the market place. Think of them as the god father and god mother of mortgage rules and lending requirements.

25) YOUR DOGS

They'll be fine.

26) YOUR KIDS

They'll be fine. Get them packed, get them their own room, get them excited.

27) YOUR FAMILY

Don't listen to them. Just invite them over once you close!

As you can see, the above list is just to name a lot of the parties involved. Sometimes there are contractors, attorneys, and other outside parties involved to some capacity in your transaction. While there are many moving parts, I always recommend molding into someone's team. In order to select your team, you first have to select your go-to person for the transaction. I, more often than not, am my client's go-to, where I refer them to the above necessary parties, hence the phrase "the Mortgage Quarterback." I have spent the last 10 years finding the right service providers for both myself and my clients. Thus, it is easy to refer based on client's needs and personalities, to the correct people I see best suited to work well together and get the job done.

Keep in mind; everyone has the same goal in mind, which is to CLOSE THE DEAL. Emotions run high, personalities conflict, attorneys think they are always right, the bank asks for 101 repetitive documents, I get it, trust me, no one gets more frustrated at times than I do, until I remember, it's just a game, and the game, is real estate and mortgages.

Now, some fun facts on Realtors…

REALTOR® Demographics

- 65% percent of REALTORS® are licensed as sales agents, 22% hold broker licenses, and 15% hold broker associate licenses.
- The typical REALTOR® is a 53 year old white female who attended college and is a homeowner.
- 63% of all REALTORS® are female, and the median age of all REALTORS® is 53.
- Real estate experience of all REALTORS® (median): 10 years
- Median tenure at present firm (all REALTORS®): 4 years
- Most REALTORS® worked 40 hours per week in 2016.
- The median gross income of REALTORS® was $42,500 in 2016, an increase from $39,200 in 2015.
- Formal education of REALTORS®:
  - Some college: 31%
  - Bachelor's degree: 31%
  - Graduate degree and above: 13%
  - Associate degree: 12%
  - Some graduate school: 6%
  - High school graduate: 7%
- REALTOR® affiliation with firms:
  - Independent contractor: 86%
  - Employee: 5%
  - Other: 9%

Source: 2017 National Association of REALTORS® Member Profile

Tip #56
Always check to see the legality of a house. Make sure a 3 family is really a legal 3 family.

CHAPTER 11:

FUNNY MONEY STORIES

6 Funniest Mortgage Memories…

That the Mortgage Quarterback can recall.

Over a decade you think you can hear it all and see it all. But let me just pre-warn you, this article may leave you in tears from crying at the most ridiculous and absurd stories dating back to December 2007.

I won't be giving names, just scenarios. I can assure you, you will be highly entertained.

These stories are NOT in the funniest order.

1.   My client, who was a barber, brought $25,000 of cash in a brown paper bag to the closing table as his "down payment money." When we all asked, "Hey, what's in the bag?", he replied, "my down payment money I have been saving for the last few weeks…" Meanwhile, we have bank statements showing more than that with seasoned funds (funds that have been in a bank for more than 90 days). Needless to say, we all know a barber doesn't make

> **Tip #57**
>
> Always check the basement for mold.
>
> **Tip #58**
>
> If you want the lowest rate, have the highest credit score.

THAT much cutting hair in "A few weeks" and that he had to go to his bank and get a certified check from his verified account.

2.   "Oh Hey Mr. Realtor, thank you for calling me." Jeff says. "Jeff, can you please let us know what you think my client will qualify for on 123 ABC Street in the Bronx?" "Sure, I can do that... it is showing as 3 stories, I can't determine if it is a 2 family, or a 3 family, can you tell me what you believe it is best used as since there is no certificate of occupancy?" Realtor replies, "well Jeff I think its a two and a half family." (My phone disconnects)

3.   "Hey Jeff, I want to bring my cousin in to help her get pre-approved" "Sure, no problem, Wednesday at 8pm, I am there" I said. "Great, just do me a favor, if you talk to any one in my family, don't tell them I saw you because you know, people get too curious" "Sure man, no problem, not saying a word" That night, at 7:55Pm, I look out my window to see my client sucking face (making out, kissing, whatever) with this unknown female. Moments later, door opens, "Hey Jeff, meet my cousin $%^*#@!" "Hey, you guys totally look alike, you must be very closely related" I said.

4.   "Jeff, do you mind if I bring my family with me to the pre-approval meeting?" "Sure, bring whoever you want..." In rolls 13 family members, grandma, grandpa, mom, dad, brother, brother, brother, and 5 kids. Needless to say, the office was a ZOO!

5.   "Hey Joe, here are the documents we are going to need. 2012/2013 tax returns, 2012/2013 w2 forms, two most recent pay stubs, bank statements from the previous month, driver

license…" "Ok, great, I will see you Monday." Monday rolls around and in comes Joe, with a backpack. I thought it was a bit strange and full, but hey, to each his own. Joe then pulls out an entire stack of paper… what was it? 104 pay stubs. He misread the email. Thought we need 2 years worth of pay stubs.

6. This is one of my favorites. It's April of 2009, I am in the heat of massive business growth, and I get a call from my client crying. "Jeff, you lied to me. I have been working with you for months. I just spoke to this attorney since we are now getting our contract of sale. Him and his assistant told me not to work with you, because you are a broker, and you charge at least 2 points on every deal." "After calming her down, reassuring her that I am a direct lender, I do not charge not only any points, but no fees as well, that she is in great hands, and how could someone be so far off?" Along with that, I was able to get who the attorney was that said that stuff. I told my client I would call her back in an hour. I got in my car (a black, tinted out Denali), drove to the attorneys office in the Bronx. Pulled right up on the curb to block any one from leaving the office, jumped over the hood of my car and barged into the attorney's personal office. I am pretty sure still to this day his ears are ringing from me screaming at him. Well, it turns out, his "Assistants" brother worked for another mortgage company, and she was getting kick backs, and the attorney was getting all of their legal work. NEEDLESS TO SAY, THAT never happened again, and both apologized, and may have peed in their pants.

The residential mortgage business is quite hysterical to be a part of on a daily basis. The amount of EMOTION that is involved from all parties is beyond imaginable. I invite you all reading this to come spend a day, or an hour with me and see what we go through. You will laugh, cringe, and confirm that you do NOT want to sit in my seat, haha. But, you will learn a lot, and you will be motivated to helping others, big time.

Until next time, success & happiness. GO GET IT.

Tip #59

If you have a house, you have to shovel snow. If you have a condo, the association has to shovel the snow.

CHAPTER 12:

JUST (DON'T) DO IT!

Run your credit after you apply for a mortgage, until after you close.

Deposit cash into your bank account, other than checks or pay earned

Transfer money around

Quit your job

Leave your job and move without telling anyone

Lie about anything on your application

Stop paying your bills

Stop paying your rent

Max out credit cards

Make any larger purchases with debt

Get divorced and not tell us

Provide false documentation

Change your name

By not doing the above, you will have a smooth sailing process! If you do any of

---

Tip #60

Follow the US 10 YR treasury note to track interest rate trends.

Tip #61

Check different areas to purchase property. Don't settle on one town, one price point. Change it up.

the above, your loan may not get approved and will cause frustration for all parties.

Housing Inventory is SLOWING down the Real Estate Market.

The Screeching HALT.

No, not screech from that old TV show…

In mid-2017 I consulted with many of my real estate, legal, and insurance friends in the industry and they have all said the same thing, "It has gotten very quiet with new deal flow." My team and I have seen a slower loan submission (new loans entering processing) than normal. Is the market losing momentum or what's the deal?

There are always a number of reasons for worry and concern, but then there is just history repeating itself. Let's look at some of my viewpoints on the current state of the market as of July 22, 2017.

1.   It's just that. It's JULY 22nd. The people that wanted to move for summer, did already. They bought their house between MAY & June, and some lingered around until July. July is the vacation month of the year. There is no school, the full month can be dedicated to family time, travel time, and letting your hair down time. Business has always slowed down in July since 2007 when I got into the business.

2.   Homes for sale right now are over priced. Probably 90% of the homes sitting for sale on the market right now are asking way above their current value. How do I know this? This past month, my team and I had 4 properties under appraise, because homes were sold at prices higher than their current

worth, essentially the buyer paying a premium. The closed sales data has not caught up the rising market prices.

3.   Quality homes are not for sale. Many of the homes I have viewed are out dated. The kitchens are yellow, the bathrooms are pink, and the grass needs to be cut. The problem is, the neighbors home just sold for a lot, and the seller thinks their home is better because "they have been there for 25+ years", oh yeah, and they also don't have the money to make the repairs or upgrades needed to help them get top dollar for their home.

Where are we going? DUDE! Where are we going?

1.   Well, new inventory (condos specifically) will be hitting the market for sale. If you look all around Hudson County and New York City (Manhattan/Queens/Brooklyn particularly) there is construction everywhere. Drive down any street in the city and you'll see what I am talking about. Yes, a lot of these are rentals, but who cares; there's an ass for every seat.

2.   Debt consolidation will be at an all-time high. Every single industry I consult with has a ridiculous amount of debt. Everyone and their mother has borrowed with low interest rates. We will experience another interest rate drop in order to refinance people into lower monthly payments, allowing them to re-afford their astronomical amount of debt.

Tip #62
Ask your parents if they will tap into their home equity to partner with you on your first purchase.

3.   ALL THE WAY UP. Prices will run 15 percent plus from now

until year end. Mark my words. Based on the trends I have seen for the last 30 days alone, this market is not stopping. Think of a rocket ship to the moon, non-stop.

Blast off for prices.

4. Alternative Financing will hit a new all-time high. As banks continue to break balls left and right, people will pay higher rates for investments in return for sanity and less paperwork and verification having to be provided.

FOLLOW THE MONEY. Not the yellow brick road.

Wall Streeters and Hedge Funds have left stocks and bonds to focus on REAL ESTATE & High Interest REAL ESTATE LOANS. This means, they know something a lot of us don't know. Which is, I will share with you, we are in a METRO-NYC area housing shortage. There are more people needing to live here than there are current dwellings/units for sale or for rent. Supply and demand drives prices up.

Finally, I keep my market forecast at buy REAL ESTATE, all of it, for the next 17 months now. Rates will remain low, if not go lower, prices will go up, through the roof, and you will make a killing. Save money in the mean time. Don't waste it on meaningless things that give you no return. We are at a very solid point in the market and we all need to take advantage of it.

BUY a Home, REfinance your current debt, start a business, and have FUN, man. It's all about FUN and doing the right thing.

CHAPTER 13:
21 QUESTIONS (WITH ANSWERS!)

1. What documents will you need to "purchase a home"?

If you are getting a mortgage, I recommend getting together the past 2 years federal tax returns, w2 forms, two most recent month's bank statements, all accounts, all pages, driver license and social security card, and 2 most recent pay stubs. If you get this list together, you are 99% ready to start. If you are NOT getting a mortgage, simply gather your driver license, and most recent month's bank statements to show funds available, to buy the real estate, with your cash. Between pre-approval and closing, you can and most definitely will be asked for MORE documents, depending on many factors. I recommend you understanding and accepting this from day 1. The bank has 12+ difference compliance sectors to answer to, and banks are afraid of making mistakes, and I am the first to say it, it is NOT easy, and the government makes it harder each day.

2. What are the qualifying guidelines?

This is a great question, and guidelines change based on loan types. There are three main loan types, FHA, Conventional, and VA (Veterans loans). Your credit score, income, property type purchasing, cash available, and occupancy (Whether you are buying an investment or place to live in) all impact guidelines. I

> **Tip #63**
>
> Everyone's loan is different. Worry about your loan.. not anyone else's loan.

would be happy to educate you specific to YOUR best loan for YOU, and go into detail.

3. Am I ready at this point in my life to BUY my 1st Place?

YES. You are always ready to make an investment. Rates are relatively low, and property values will keep going up. I always recommend my clients (if they are worried) to buy a place that they know that they can rent out in the immediate future for a break even on what rent they will get minus their mortgage. For example, if your mortgage is $2,000 per month, you need to make sure you are able to rent the place for at least $2,000 per month, this way if you are not happy and need to move, you can do so and still have the investment and take advantage of the tax benefits, without losing money. Now is the BEST time to buy. You will be worried and have fear, but with the right team, it'll get done.

4. How do I fix things myself?

Easy items to be fixed such as lighting or a faucet do it. Painting? Do it. When it comes to bigger issues like drains, pipes, windows, electrical outlets, etc, always hire a contractor / handy man. Everyone knows someone who does this type of work. Before hiring the person, get a FREE quote in writing, along with a detailed explanation. Like all industries, many contractors are unreliable and desperate, and over charge the uneducated consumer.

5. Interest Rates—What is my monthly payment?

Although the payment is VERY important, interest rates change by the second. I always give my clients a three-month range of where rates are and have been, within .5%, so 3.75% to 4.25%

as an example. If you are in contract to purchase a home, then rates become more accurate, but if you are "just looking" always use the higher range for worst case scenario. Your monthly payment is unable to be calculated until you find a home and confirm your final loan amount. Your payment is comprised of your mortgage, your real estate taxes, and your insurances, all of which are variable until later on in the process.

6.   What can I easily afford?

This is different for everyone. Everyone has different expenses in life, such as kids, private schools, gas, tolls, food, spending habits. I recommend my clients keeping their mortgage payment in the range of 33% of their GROSS monthly income. If you make $120,000 per year, that is $10,000 per month, which 33% of that, would put you at a payment no higher than $3,300, which includes the same taxes and insurances, and mortgage.

7.   Do I want to be locked into this area?

You are never locked in to any area to live. To own, you may be. Meaning, you may have to hold on to the property, and I don't ever recommend selling property, ever, unless you have to because you need the money. Worst case, move out and rent again, or call your parents up and tell them "I'm coming Home." I don't know many people that ever sold real estate and lost money.

8.   What does the location look like during the day, night, and weekend?

Excellent question, also factor in the

> **Tip #64**
>
> Interest rates change by the second.
>
> **Tip #65**
>
> Be realistic in your home search. Let your realtor guide you home.

time of year, parking, kids out of school. The only answer is spending some time there during those times. It may be harder to do and wait during time of year, but drive around before and after work, on weekends, and early in the changing of seasons. This will give you an accurate understanding of the area.

9.   What's the likeliness of making money on the property?

I never recommend you calculating your investment or profit on a place you are moving into. This should be your happy place. If you make money one day, GREAT. If you are happy where you live, that is the GOAL! However, to answer the question, you will make money immediately with the tax benefit (speak to an accountant or CPA), and in this market, home prices are rising anywhere from 1%-6% per year, depending on the location. If you buy now, worst-case scenario, 18 months from now, you will have made instant equity, which is the difference between the purchase price and the new valuation.

10.   Do I need to consider the area for future plans?

Marriage, kids, etc. Depending on where you are in life, age, relationship, finances, career, you may want to spend some time making your "first move", however, things change, plans change, and areas change. I have always believed in being one of the first frontiers into an area, based on my experience. Many people are turning towards easy Urban living, where you can walk to the corner store, park, ball fields, etc., so to be clear, your personal current situation will dictate how much time you spend looking into schools, house size, etc.

11.   What does my loan amount look like?

Everyone has their own process, and my recommendation works for me, and has worked for thousands of clients like yourself. Let US, the professionals guide you, and you make the final COMFORTABLE decision on final numbers and payments. We ask to get all of your documents to my team, and then they do the data entry of your information, run your credit, and insert all of the relative information. I then review the information and provide an A to Z analysis of what I see. Every client gets this, and Rebekah and Zack put their input in as well. Your loan amount should be conservative if possible, but most importantly, AFFORDABLE.

12.   How does cash impact your decision?

Me Personally, I would rather have more cash in the bank and a higher mortgage payment. As a pure example, if you were able to keep $25,000 in the bank, and have a higher monthly payment of $200, who cares? $25,000 in an account, divided by $200 in payment, you have over 10 years of the difference in payment saved up. I would set a direct transfer every month into my bills pay account, and not even realize the payment was higher. This is just me, but cash is king, so save as much as you can while having an affordable mortgage payment.

13.   What about Savings Bonds and Investments, other ASSets like that?

Other assets are great. However, I NEVER recommend selling tax

> **Tip #66**
>
> Make your budget first, then worry about buying a home.
>
> **Tip #67**
>
> You do not need to file your taxes by April 15... File an extension.

implicated assets for a home. Keep them in their asset class, for as long as possible. I would look to take money from a 401k loan, or increase my tax with holdings from my pay stubs to get more money per paycheck, to save my down payment. Why pay tax on money previously taxed? It doesn't make sense to me at all. But I am different and think differently. Remember that!

14.   When do you ask family for HELP?

Never. Unless it is required. If you need a few thousand dollars to qualify, ask. If you can make the mortgage payment comfortably, but have student loans your parents may be paying, ask for co-signer help from them. It is much more rewarding doing it on your own, Trust me. YOU DID IT! I am not against or opposed to help or a safety net, but I would save that option unless 100% needed.

15.   If you are in need of a co-signer, do they own the property?

Yes, technically, if your lawyer structures it that way. I would recommend getting a non-occupying (co borrower does not live in property) co-signer and have an exit strategy in mind (how to get them off the mortgage and be removed as a co-signer) so that you have a time frame and game plan in mind. I love structuring these types of deals; they are fun and need my creativity to plan this out.

16.   What documents does a Co-signer need?

The same ones you would need as above. A co-borrower, co-signer, or borrower all are viewed as equal and are all legally responsible on the mortgage. If you miss a payment, their credit gets hit with a late payment. There is a TON of risk being a co-borrower, co-signer. I do not recommend it, unless needed, and keep in mind; you need to have a game plan again to get them off the loan!

17.   Buy vs Rent—WHY?

Buying is an investment, but should not be viewed as one. You have an asset, you can sell the asset. You are building wealth, and home ownership is the American dream. Prices have gone up where some people have the American nightmare, but being properly educated and making a calculated risk decision will work out for you. If you buy today, I guarantee you in 10-20 years you will have made money on your investment. Renting is not a bad option, but you are paying someone else's mortgage. I actually rented for 4 years, and owned 3 properties as investments, since I didn't know where I wanted to live, while in New York, and always knew I would be back in JERSEY, eventually. I rented in Hoboken for 2.5 years, to learn the area, lend money in the area, and begin seeing trends. Let my experience and vision assist you in your decision-making.

18.   Should I put 20% down?

Yes, in some cases, but you don't *have* to. I would always rather my clients putting less money down. In today's market, you can put 1% down payment, or 3.5% down payment, or 5% down payment, as low options. Some of these options do have MORTGAGE INSURANCE, but who cares, you are saving money. Again, affordability is KEY. I have some options for first time homebuyers where you can put less

Tip #68

If you don't buy one of the first ten properties you see, you're either not ready or your realtor isn't hearing your needs.

than 20% down, and avoid paying monthly mortgage insurance. Just ask me how.

19.   How do my current debts impact where I stand?

This is a great question and I personally have a major issue with how the government calculates income and debts. They purposely exclude DEBTS that are real. It makes no sense, so what I do is offer my clients a free budget analysis, and review all of their bank statements and check their spending habits, so I can best advise on the best move and loan type. Most clients are private and don't want this, but the ones that take me up on my offer are much better financially positioned and clear on their decision to purchase. I am not just your "mortgage guy" I am the guy that is and always will be in your corner, your rock, and your go-to for important decisions.

20.   Who do you trust in the process and Why?

Myself, haha. ME, I. There are so many pretenders and uneducated, unethical, inexperienced "professionals" in the market that make it VERY difficult and unnecessary difficult to buy a home. There are over 17 people needed in your transaction to have you finally buy a home, 13 of which you will never meet or talk to. We can get into this later, but my recommendation is use someone you trust and get them to implement their team. I am ALL about TEAM. I have my own attorneys, insurance people, realtors, accountants, and I can assure you, my team is the best, most ethical, honorable, and real people out there. If you know me, I don't like pretenders, and if you are a real player, you play and do business with REAL players. Can someone mess up or make a mistake, absolutely, human error, but HONEST mistakes. I would look to deal with people that have a proven system and track record to work together and accomplish the goal of helping you buy your home, close the deal, and stay in touch as a lifelong client forever.

21.   What is your #1 TIP for the 30 years young and younger generation?

Get off your butt, find your passion, lock into a career where you feel wanted, needed, fulfilled and PASSIONATE about going to work every day. COMMIT. SAVE MONEY. Set yourself up for a fantastic future. Get 1 or 2 friends together, like yourself, and buy a house with them. Pay off your debt. Live stress free, as much as possible. Take calculated RISK. Learn from me, my experiences, my valuable mistakes. Get a role model, push your limits, Never Give UP.

CHAPTER 14:

FEEDBACK FROM A MILLENNIAL REAL ESTATE INVESTOR/ENTREPRENEUR

"Jeff and I were the same age when we met back in 2010. I honestly thought he was full of crap but after doing some research I realized this kid was the real deal. If it wasn't for Jeff, I wouldn't be in the position I am in today as he led me in the right direction and showed me how to make the right moves in regards to financing to help keep me with money in pocket and reach my goals of buying properties every year since then. I have now done 9 mortgages with Jeff and his team and I now have 1 primary residence and 7 investment properties."—Mike D'Annucci, Bronx NY, Department of Transportation

Some advice from Mike:

The population keeps growing every day but the land doesn't grow ever. Buy something now while the population grows and so will your value of what you buy.

When buying property, set a goal and determine what this property and how this property will be beneficial to you. There is no wrong answer as each individual has their own perspective on a property; it's all about how it works for you and your money.

Some examples from Mike:

1) Living rent-free with a multi-family. Have tenants help pay some, if not all, of your mortgage.

2) Flipping a property just buying cheap and knowing you have buyers that will pay more for it, such as auctions or foreclosures.

3) Renovate a property at cost if you're good at construction and flip it for a profit.

4) Fully rent a property to make a return on your investment or take out a shorter period of loan (15 year loan opposed to 30 years) so it gets paid off and you have supplemental income, or retire and collect rent.

5) Owning your own business and running it from your multi-family property. Work where you live and own.

6) Buy a multi-family and divide the mortgage payment amongst your family. Say you buy a 3 family, grandparents on the bottom, parents on the middle floor, you on top.

Nothing is easy in real estate. The key is planning and having a strong network to deliver for you. No matter what your plan is, always have a backup plan.

Tip #69

Stop making excuses. Take the necessary steps to improve your financial profile.

CHAPTER 15:

REAL ESTATE APPRAISALS EXPLAINED, BY MIKE CONTE OF NATIONWIDE PROPERTY & APPRAISAL SERVICES

In today's lending environment there are three key components that determine a borrower's eligibility for securing a mortgage. They are credit, income and assets. The home that you own or wish to buy is the biggest asset in a mortgage transaction. It is the collateral that lending institutions rely on to mitigate risk while providing a borrower the money they need for a purchase or refinance. Mortgages can range from a few thousand dollars into the tens of millions, with that kind of money on the line it is important to understand how a property's value is determined.

There are three "approaches" a real estate appraiser will use when accessing market value. They are the sales comparison, income and cost approach. Each approach will conclude what a home is worth based on a different set of underlying factors.

The cost approach is a real estate valuation method that surmises that the price a buyer should pay for a piece of property should equal the cost to build an equivalent building. In a cost approach appraisal, the market price for the property is equal to the cost of land plus cost of construction, less depreciation.

The income approach is a real estate appraisal method that allows investors to estimate the value of a property by taking the net operating income of the rent collected and dividing it by the capitalization rate.

The sales comparison approach compares recently sold local similar properties to the subject property. Price adjustments are made for differences in the comparable and subject property. When it comes to financing a residential property intended as a primary residence the sales comparison approach is king. All lending decisions will be based on this number.

So how exactly does a bank determine this value, it starts with the real estate appraiser. A real estate appraiser is a specially licensed and trained individual whose sole job is to determine the value of residential and commercial real estate. They are an independent neutral third party that acts as the eyes and ears for the bank. Because they have no vested interest in the property banks rely heavily on their opinion. Their onsite inspection and local market expertise will shape the very foundation of your mortgage financing. A high or low value can impact the amount of money you can borrow and the interest rate you will be charged.

Right now you should be asking yourself, "What can I do to improve the value of my home and secure the best available financing"? Let's start with the basics.

Tidy up! It amazes me to no end how many appraisal reports I have seen where the home is in complete disarray. Dirty laundry on the floor and bed, dishes stacked ceiling high in the sink, shrubs and lawn completely overgrown, the list goes on and on. There is no excuse for any of this and if you think for one minute the appraiser's opinion of your home is not

Tip #70
An hourly wage earner is different than a salary wage earner.

adversely affected by this mess you are sorely mistaken. The same reason realtors spend thousands of dollars staging a new listing should be the same reason why you tidy up your home, to attract top dollar! Pretend your relatives are coming over for Thanksgiving dinner and get your home looking it's best. Best of all it's completely free to do, just requires a little elbow grease.

Next step, tackle all the "deferred maintenance". Deferred maintenance is a term appraisers use to address items that are incomplete or long overdue for some attention. Think of your car, every 3,000 miles you need to change the oil. If you haven't changed the oil in 10,000 miles your car isn't going to run right and it's value is going to drop, same thing with your house. The biggest culprit in regards to deferred maintenance is interior and exterior paint. Painted surfaces need to be repainted over the years to keep them looking their best and help protect the integrity of the underlying materials.

Other deferred maintenance can include resurfacing a driveway, powerwashing a shed, steam cleaning old carpets or staining a wood deck. Odds are you already know which handy man projects require your attention, what better motivation to get them done than to save money on your mortgage.

By tackling these two steps you can increase the value of your home and eliminate the need for any secondary inspections. A "final inspection" may be necessary if an appraiser finds items that would prevent a home from meeting Fannie Mae or FHA guidelines. These items would need to be remedied and then a second inspection would be required to show the requested work has been completed. A time \-wasting hassle for sure but also an expensive one as each final inspection will cost you $150 - $250.

Even if your home is clean with no signs of deferred maintenance you may still face a final inspection for various other reasons. To be the odds and avoid a final inspection follow the checklist below.

- Have smoke and CO detectors installed and in working order

- All utilities should be on including water, electric and gas (if the home has gas)

- HVAC systems and kitchen appliances should all be functioning properly

- Depending on your state (typically those prone to earthquakes like CA) your hot water heater needs to be double strapped

- There should be no signs of active remodeling like a half finished bathroom, etc. The home should be in one piece and fully functional

- Make all rooms of the home accessible for the appraiser including attics, basements, crawl spaces, sheds and garages.

We've all watched the shows on HGTV like "Flip or Flop" and "Property Brothers" where savvy real estate investors turn neglected homes into works of art and make a nice profit along the way. Besides tidying up and addressing signs of deferred maintenance nothing increases a home's worth like remodeling can. Money spent on kitchens and bathrooms can go a long way to improve a home's value. So can new floors, windows, roofing, siding, HVAC and landscaping. These options are more expensive and time consuming but could make or break a

Tip #71

Find out immediately if there are violations on a property you want to purchase.

purchase or refinance.

Now that your home is looking good and you've taken all the necessary steps to avoid a final inspection it's time for the appraiser to come do his inspection. If you've followed my advice this process should be nothing more than a formality. The appraiser will walk the entire property and take lots of measurements and photographs to properly document the home. Once this is done we return back to the "sales comparison approach" we discussed above.

The appraiser is going to formulate an opinion of value based on available data and local market expertise. The best source of data comes from recently sold homes in the immediate market area, commonly referred to as "comps." These are your comparable sales that give the best indication of what your home is worth. This process can be more complicated than one might think since most neighborhoods have all different styles of homes with various differences in amenities such as lot size, bedroom and bathroom count, age, gross living area, garages, basements, fireplaces, pools, decks and most importantly, condition. Adjustments need to be made for all of these amenities line by line. Very rarely will an appraiser be able to make an apples to apples comparison from one home to another. With so many variables to consider there is typically some adjustments that need to take place.

Once an appraiser has found at least three suitable comps they will formulate an opinion of value after each property has been properly adjusted. They will bracket their value using those sales. For example if Comps 1, 2 and 3 sold for $340,000, $352,000 and $365,000 respectively after adjustments you should expect your sales comparison approach value to fall somewhere between $340,000 and $365,000. The final determination will depend on which sales are given the most weight. Typically the sales that are the most recent with the least adjustments that are closest in proximity will have the greatest impact.

Now that you understand what an appraisal is and how it works into your mortgage application let's apply this knowledge to the real world, specifically a purchase transaction. A purchase can't occur until a property owner decides they want to sell their home. Whatever the motivation for selling might be you can bet securing a high sales price is a top priority. This is where having the right team comes in to play and for a seller that means partnering with the right listing agent. Deciding on the right listing agent can be a daunting task. They will be managing every aspect of the sale from start to finish. Needless to say this is a major responsibility and one that comes with a huge financial impact. Beware of Realtors promising numbers that are too good to be true. The right Realtor will be very familiar with the appraisal process and be able to lay out a factual representation of what your home should sell for. Listing your home for sale well above those numbers is a recipe for disaster because one of two things will happen.

One, your home will sit on the market untouched. It will be ignored by realtors and prospective buyers alike, and if nobody is walking in the door to look at your home your chances of a sale are zero. Maybe you are not in a rush to sell but this approach still has consequences. Once you reprice the home lower to attract more attention people will still notice how long it has been on the market. The longer the property has sat on the MLS the more buyers start to think, "Why is this home still listed for sale, something must be wrong with it."

Tip #72
Review your credit report with your lender. Make sure everything is accurate.

Tip #73
PMI is much less these days... avoid 20% down.

The second thing that might happen if you list too high can be emotionally so much more painful. Let's just say by some miracle you actually attract a buyer to purchase your overpriced home. You may be thinking "well look at me, I'm a genius. I'm going to make a fortune selling my house, haha." Not so fast my friend, remember that home appraisal we talked about, it's back! Your buyer is going to need to secure a mortgage unless they have all cash to buy the home outright. Regardless of the purchase price you and the buyer agreed upon the bank is only going to lend on what the home appraises for. Remember the home is the collateral the bank secures their money too. If the mortgage holder stops making their payments the bank will repossess the house and the only way they are going to get their money back is by selling the home to a new buyer at fair market value. Just because your buyer was willing to overpay doesn't mean anybody else will and the bank knows this. They will cap the purchase price based on the sales comparison approach. You will have to either renegotiate the purchase price based on the appraisal or convince the buyers to cover the overage with cash. The bank will certainly allow you to overpay but it will be with your money not theirs.

This scenario rarely has a happy ending. Once buyers see they are overpaying they will seldom be willing to continue through with the transaction at the originally agreed upon price. Both parties have seen their hopes crushed while wasting a lot of time and money along the way, and for what? A well-trained listing agent would have seen this coming and steered you away from this mistake before the home ever hit the market.

Regardless if you are a buyer or seller, make sure your Realtor understands the appraisal process and has the factual data from step one to negotiate the proper sales price. The bank and home appraiser will not be fooled, and neither should you.

A refinance works much the same way except now you already own the home. No realtors are involved; it's only you and your loan officer. If you thought choosing the right Realtor was important it pales in comparison to working with the right loan officer. A savvy and well-educated loan officer is critical for securing the best mortgage terms AND more importantly, actually getting the loan closed. As someone who has closed tens of millions of dollars in mortgages prior to my career in Appraisal Management I can tell you with complete confidence that the right loan officer makes all the difference. There are pitfalls around every corner, the appraisal process certainly being one of them. An experienced loan officer will see these coming and avoid them at all costs. There are hundreds of loan programs each with their own underwriting guidelines. Knowing the ins and outs of each program takes intelligence, time and expertise. A truly great loan officer will discuss and educate you every step of the way.

CHAPTER 16:

NOW KNOW YOUR NUMBERS

It is very important that you understand your money, what you are bringing in and what you are putting out. Banks only take into account your guaranteed payments that they know of when qualifying you. These guaranteed payments are anything on your credit report showing the minimum payment, any alimony or child support you have to pay (hopefully you don't have to pay or receive any) along with your student loans. In order to calculate your payments on your student loans please consult with a licensed mortgage loan originator to keep up to date with guidelines, as all mortgage loans have specific calculation requirements. Here are some OTHER bills you want to factor in when getting a mortgage, and the numbers used below are strictly an example, as is the proposed income, for you to properly understand.

Let's say you make $120,000 per year, which equates to $10,000 per month.

$10,000 per month Gross pay

Subtract all of your deductions for health insurance, 401k, etc. and now you bring home $6,000

I recommend taking 30% of your gross income to budget for your new mortgage, which keep in mind, includes your mortgage payment of principal and interest, real estate taxes, home insurance, and PMI.

So, you subtract $3,000 from your $6,000 take home pay.

Add up the following:

Cable Bill	$	Clothes Shopping	$
Auto Insurance	$	Month Subscriptions	$
Electric Bill	$	Gym Memberships	$
Food	$	Holiday Gifts	$
Cell Phone	$	Professional Services	$
Gas/Tolls	$	Insurance Co-Pay	$
Life Insurance	$	Kid's School	$
Private Loan	$	Cleaning Service	$
Wireless Internet	$	Personal Upkeep	$
Other	$	Other	$
Grand Total:	$		

CHAPTER 17:

FINAL TIPS

If you are buying a condo, don't just check the condo itself, make sure the home owner's association has sufficient reserve funds, and there are not too many delinquent home owners'. Always get a condo questionnaire filled out by the managing agent or company prior to submitting your mortgage application, or simultaneously. There is often a fee associated with this, and this is money well spent.

Do NOT shop for the cheapest attorney. Your attorney's fee is the best money spent. Your attorney is to protect you. Find an attorney that charges a flat fee, competitive with market rates, and put your trust in him or her to guide you home. Do not question every item, as there are many moving parts to a real estate transaction.

TRUST THE PROCESS. This means to rely on all of your service providers. Pick your go-to person to rely on; whether it is your mortgage lender, attorney, or realtor, stick with them, they have your best interest in mind.

Do not ask or email the bank every day for status.

Be patient. I know emotions run high and you are anxious, excited, worried, nervous and probably can't sleep. Everyone has the same goal in mind, to help you close the deal as quickly as possible, and most cost effectively as possible.

Do not over shop. Regardless of what lender, attorney, or insurance provider you use, find someone you trust, read their reviews, ask a friend, relative or co-worker, and go with someone that is recommended to you. The more you shop and grind someone down on price, the less attention the service provider will give to you. You get what you pay for. I would rather pay a little bit extra for an industry expert, to put on my team for the rest of my life, rather than get the cheapest service provider, with the worst service and probably limited knowledge.

Always get a home inspection.

Always check to see if the home or condo you are buying is in a flood zone, ask your lender. If you are buying all-cash without a mortgage, ask a lender or your realtor.

Expect to provide the bank you use multiple documents, multiple times. Expect the worst.

Remember, people are people and humans make mistakes. Nobody is perfect, so be understanding of those involved in the transaction. Everyone is in the business to help achieve the same goal.

If you are buying a vacant house, a bank owned property or short sale, always make sure the heat and water are turned on and work. If pipes don't run or the boiler isn't turned on for quite some time, there is a chance they could be broken and you don't even know. It is better to be safe than sorry. Make sure when you walk through the house, you flush all of the toilets, run all of the faucets, and open all of the windows and doors to make sure all work and there are not any leaks, bugs, or mold.

Tip #74

A home inspection report is not a requirement, but definitely recommended.

Tip #75

Don't worry how bad your credit is. It can always be fixed.

Don't be petty with your negotiations. Anything under $2,000, don't grind the seller down on.

No home is perfect. Be realistic. Put yourself in the seller's shoes.

Always request electric and heating bills from the seller so you can know what to expect for when you buy the home or condo.

Always check the roof.

Always follow the market for news, trends, and tips to stay up to date with what is going on.

Rely on those who have a proven track record.

Don't listen to someone who bought their house 5, 10 or 15 years ago. The entire game has changed and all of the rules were rewritten.

You should never pay any monies out of pocket prior to closing other than a deposit for the down payment, your inspection fee, your appraisal fee, or maybe a retainer fee for your lawyer. If anyone asks you for money, consult with your go-to person. If your go-to person asks you for money, find another go-to person!

Have your lender check your credit. A lender credit report and any free credit report out there will be showing different scores. I have seen sometimes the free reports are higher and sometimes lower. Since the lender is the one who will be lending you money, use their report and trust the accuracy of it, as it is the best report out there.

Just because you are buying a home for a certain price, doesn't mean your home is worth that price. A good example of this is the following. A lady was buying a house for $500,000, which she won in a bidding war. The property was listed at $450,000, and she paid

$50,000 more. She chose to pay a premium due to the lack of supply, and heavy demand in the market. A lender will only lend on the appraised value. An appraisal is defined as an opinion of value.

If you are buying a house for a certain price, the appraiser will not try to appraise the house higher than the contract price. Once the appraiser meets the value of the contract, legally, he or she will likely stop there and get the appraisal back in to the lender's hands to have your loan approval be worked on. This doesn't mean your house isn't worth more, it just means the appraiser is doing his job for LENDING purposes only.

If you have a judgment or collections, pay them.

If you have any skeletons in your closet, tell your lender up front so a solution can be implemented before the process gets serious.

Submit all of your documents in full. Do not piece mail.

GET in the GAME! When the game is real estate & mortgages.

Game, ON.

A Real Estate Letter to Millennials.

The WHY behind people older than you…

I have been looking for an image to properly depict, from my perspective of course, what 2008 really looked like.

Great, now that you have seen that image, of the entire real estate market being on fire, smoking, and up in flames, check out the second image below.

I was unable to find, and didn't feel like making my own image, that added "AND HAVE NO MONEY FOR YOU," to the picture of the Bank, "Sorry we're closed" image.

Many Americans, specifically previous home owners, and even renters for that matter, are still scarred from 2008. I am assuming they still ask themselves the question "Is history going to repeat itself" and "Am I going to lose 60% of my net worth again over night" and possibly "would I be able to physically, mentally, emotionally, and financially be able to survive if a 2008-like crisis happened ever again?"

JEFF VAN NOTE

Dear Millennials,

I write this letter to you to explain the mind set of older people, older generations, and detail what they lived through, so that YOU are able to inspire them, motivate them, and have empathy towards them, for what they have been through.

If you touch the hot stove and get burned, more likely than not, you will not touch it ever again, whether it is hot or cold, or you will likely be hesitant and slowly lower your hand to begin to feel for heat. YOUR parents, YOUR bosses, YOUR mentors, YOUR older friends, and YOUR mailman, doctor, bus driver, survived the economic collapse of 2008. Their 401k accounts went from $100,000, to $40,000 literally over night. Their home value went from $400,000, to $200,000, their credit cards that had open limits of $25,000, were closed out. Their home equity line of credit that was $250,000 open limit, was dropped to $50,000, and frozen.

If you don't understand the above, let me explain to you the trickle down impact. Their 401k was supposed to be their down payment on their home. 60% of it disappeared, now they weren't able to borrow the funds to use for a down payment. Their home value dropping from $400,000 to $200,000 crushed their possibilities of selling their home... because they had a $375,000 mortgage on it, leaving them with 2 options, stop paying the mortgage and move, or stay put and pay a loan of $375,000 on an asset worth about $200,000. Their credit cards had limits of $25,000 were closed out without notice, and they had planned to pay your first semester of college with the credit card, or birthday presents, or Christmas presents, or repair the boiler in their home, now they couldn't. Finally, their $250,000 line of credit was there to make significant improvements to your home, so that everyone could have more space, the pool could be put in so you can all enjoy having friends over and swimming, and the

146

basement could be finished for you and your friends to have your own space for loud sleep overs.

People who have not been through financial distress, investment losses, or life change of plans and detours don't understand the negative impact on mental mindset moving forward. People get stuck in safe mode, as safe mode is better than the unknown.

It is my belief that more than 70 percent of homeowners missed at least one mortgage payment from 2007 to 2010. It is also my belief, that without family help or borrowing from friends, more people would have lost their homes. There are still many homes in the United States that haven't had their mortgage paid since 2009, maybe even 2008. Banks still are not foreclosing because they are happy with the current person living in the property paying for the electric and keeping the house monitored, so that pipes don.t burst in the winter time, and people don't break in and steal the copper pipes, or appliances, or windows.

Coming from a then 21 year old back in 2008, I saw complete wreckage, so I understand older generations protecting you from the unknowns of home ownership. I understand when they tell you to just rent, or live at home for some time. I agree with all of the advice they give, because I understand it.

> **Tip #76**
>
> When you buy real estate, get an accountant that knows real estate tax law and rules.
>
> **Tip #77**
>
> It isn't the look of the home that matters, it is the feel of the home that matters.

My goal is to properly give you advice, accurate information, and up to date education on all topics real estate related, so that you yourself can make an educated decision on home ownership. It may not be for you. Or, it may just be for you and you didn't even know or think it was possible.

I will lead you to victory of home ownership, if you have the correct, safe, educated mindset. Don't chase money, chase goals.

The great thing about real estate is even if you buy it and don't like it, you have 2 options, leave and rent it out, or sell it.

Real estate ownership doesn't have to be permanent...it is your choice.

CHAPTER 18:

CLOSING WORDS/ACKNOWLEDGEMENTS

I hope reading the previous pages gave you hope and you see opportunity in not only investing in yourself, but in your future. Over 90% of the millionaires in the country have gotten there by real estate, and over 98% of millionaires have real estate in their portfolio. In the event you are not interested in pursuing real estate as an investment, that is fine as well. I hope for you to share this book with somebody who is, even a parent or relative that could find value behind this.

I have been involved in this industry of mortgage lending and real estate, since I was 20 years old, starting in December of 2007. I have personally closed over 1,000 transactions, in multiple states, for many different types of borrowers, on many different types of real estate. By 26 years of age, I had already owned 4+ properties, completed 2 flips, and made over $1 million to myself, with nothing other than honesty, hard work, dedication, and the relentless pursuit to help others achieve the American Dream, the right way.

I sincerely look forward to hearing from you. I encourage you to follow me on social media and contact me at any given time, for my advice, my opinions, or simply just to connect. YOU are what

Tip #78
Check your bank statements and credit cards monthly.

Tip #79
Open your windows when the weather is nice to save money on your electric bill.

keeps me going and gives me life and excitement. Without you, there is no passion to be pursued.

Here's to continued and future success, whatever that may be to you!

ACKNOWLEDGMENTS

First and foremost, I would like to thank my Dad, the best role model any kid could ask for. The man who pulled the covers off of me while I was sleeping, after the first day home from college following my freshman year, demanding I get up, shave, and go to work. Thank you for teaching me how to swim at the age of 2.5 by throwing me in the deep end and telling me sink or swim, thank you for teaching me not to be afraid of a baseball by throwing them at me (Luckily you didn't have great aim) but most importantly, thank you for showing me how to be a man, handle my business, treat everyone with respect, work hard, be honest, and take care of responsibilities. I have worked my entire life trying to not only make you proud, but keep you proud. You instilled three very important things into my brain; Never Give Up, Follow your dreams, and put your head down and work. You've set the bar high and I am forever grateful. To my mother, the woman who was always there for me, supported me, drove me to every sporting event and put up with my nonsense, thank you. To my best friend, my brother Eric, Thank you for always being my number one fan. I hope you've learned from my mistakes and not a day goes by that I don't appreciate you and love you with all of my heart. To my Uncle Anthony (AC) your countless hours listening to me vent, guiding me along the proper path in life, providing me with knowledge to better myself, thank you. Your personality, voice, and smile light up my world since the day I met you when I was 8 years old. Double R, thank you for teaching me what a true friend really is. I would also like to thank every mortgage bank owner I have ever worked for, every manager I have worked alongside with, every loan processor and underwriter that had to deal with my "I don't take no for an answer" attitude, and every single client that gave me a shot, it is because of you I am able to sit here today with the most valuable knowledge and insight, thanks to you for the experience.

Please visit www.themortgagequarterback.com for up to date trends, tricks, and tips when it comes to the overall economy, real estate market, and financing options available in the market place. Stay up to date with news and interest rates that directly impact you and your investments, or future, or future investments.

Remember, it's not about what you've done; it's about what you're doing.

Made in the USA
Columbia, SC
11 August 2018